The Living Oracle

Wisdom & Divination
for
Everyday Life

The Living Oracle

Wisdom & Divination

for

Everyday Life

STEPHEN RICH MERRIMAN

Four Rivers Press

SAN FRANCISCO, CALIFORNIA

BOSTON/AMHERST, MASSACHUSETTS

www.fourriverspress.com

Book design by Tim Kinnel, www.wordsareimages.com

Cover art by Hannah Bigelow Merriman. Used by permission of the artist.

Grateful acknowledgement is made to Princeton University Press for permission to quote extensively passages from the Wilhelm/Baynes edition of
The I Ching, or Book of Changes.

ISBN 978-0-9817698-2-0

Library of Congress Control Number: 2009904331

Library of Congress subject headings:
1. Oracles. 2. Divination. 3. Wisdom.
4. Conduct of life. 5. Decision making.
6. Spiritual direction. 7. Consciousness.

To the river of consciousness that infuses the oracular traditions—past, present, and future—of all cultures, and to anyone (and everyone) who has ever posed the Jungian question:

"Who am I that these things are happening to me?"

Contents

Acknowledgements

Any book, in published form, always constitutes the culmination and fulfillment of past promises, hopes and dreams. In the course of its being fashioned, many lives cross paths with an author's, and each encounter lends a little nudge—or sometimes a major shove—to the overall force of the effort. Numerous energies always contribute to the final outcome.

In the case of *The Living Oracle: Wisdom & Divination for Everyday Life*, there were a few people who, very early on (mid-1990s) became sounding boards as some of the initial passages were taking shape. I wish to thank Vivian Walworth of Concord, Massachusetts, and Jane Goodwin and Jason Peter Williams of Cambridge, Massachusetts for extending a discriminating ear, and generous encouragement during this early period. Another person who was most valuable in this capacity was Sidney Handel, now of Tel Aviv, Israel. Sidney was a valuable confidant—and sometimes consoler—in keeping me on task with the inner work I was engaged in that prepared me to generate the passages. Also of note, I owe a significant debt of gratitude to renowned Cambridge story teller Brother Blue for his impromptu discovery—along with the courage to act on it in an utterly spontaneous, disarming and delightful way—of one solitary writer-with-notebook, sitting out under a tree in the Radcliffe Quadrangle in Cambridge, Massachusetts on a memorable late Friday afternoon in July, 1996, scribbling away on the text of Passage #24: Loneliness. That enchanting, "chance" encounter gave focus to the outcome of that passage.

A bit later in the process of the evolution of the text, there were those brave souls who volunteered to "test drive" *The*

Living Oracle by actively engaging with it. In so doing, these intrepid consulters contributed their own energy to the *Oracle*, helping to bring it to life. These individuals, friends and helpers all, include Jack Litwinsky (Cambridge, Mass.) and David Seward (Martha's Vineyard, Mass.), along with Sandra Boston, Pam Williams, Robert Place, Bill Ryan and Jeanne Lightfoot (Pioneer Valley, Western Mass.). Other Western Mass. folks to whom special thanks are due include Susan P. Lewis, who arranged for the first public presentation (including group demonstration) of *The Living Oracle* at Arms Library, Shelburne Falls, Mass. on April 12th, 2003, Janet Masucci, who extended many kindnesses to me when I was starting to explore the Pioneer Valley, Maija Meyers, for some riveting repartee, the energy of which likely shows up in several places in the passages, and Charles Quinlan of Cummington, Mass., a dear old friend of nearly forty years, and ever a true comfort.

A special thank you, along with a big hug, goes to my daughter Hannah Bigelow Merriman for her artwork, created especially for the cover of *The Living Oracle*. Hannah's interest in, and mastery of, the disciplines of astrology, the *I Ching* and the Enneagram, combined with a rich career as creative artist, were the perfect blend of sensitivities and resourcefulness for fashioning the beautiful and compelling cover image for *The Living Oracle*. I am so grateful to her for her exemplary efforts.

Thanks also to my other children, H. D. Merriman and Joely W. Merriman, for their interests in "many things oracular," one of the ongoing currencies of sharing in our family. "H. D." and Joely have each, in their own turn, contributed cover art for my previous books.

Finally, I wish to acknowledge the steadfast love and support of those who form the backbone of Four Rivers Press: first and foremost, my wife and partner Emily Sara Taylor Merriman for her love, devotion, encouragement, and that old-fashioned virtue, constancy, all combined with a prodigious knowledge and love of language; Johnn O'Sullivan, who chunked through the manuscript of *The Living Oracle*, raising with great salience occasional questions of word choice and usage, and bringing to bay many cooties that only a master copy editor could snare; and Tim Kinnel who, once again, has distinguished himself with the typesetting of the text (a very challenging task, indeed!), and the inspired creation of the look and feel of the book. Tim's efforts result in a book that is both handsome and pretty *and* eminently accessible and useful.

My gratitude is enduring to all the people I have cited, for their individual contributions which, in combined form, have brought *The Living Oracle* to its point of launch into public life—for *The Living Oracle*, a commencement—for the rest of us, the culmination of a twelve-year process.

I thank you all.

Prologue

Hunger and thirst for a sense of personal connection to Divine intention are inseparable from human striving. Every culture on earth, from at least the second millennium B.C.E. onwards, has attempted, in part, to address this yearning through the use of oracles: systems of consultation for the purpose of attaining to wisdom, guidance, and inspiration. Historically, in both Eastern and Western societies, oracular systems have found application among a broad cross-section of societal groups, regardless of the culture in which they have been developed or adapted. Oracular consultation has been employed, and relied upon, by ruling elites (secular, military or religious) as well as by intelligentsia, merchant, tradesman, commoner, serf, and peasant. In indigenous cultures, oracles have been part and parcel of shamanic enterprise, virtually the world over. In the West, the three most well known oracles which, in revised form, have evolved and come down to us across the centuries are the *I Ching*, the Tarot and the Runes.[1]

Now there is this new oracle: *The Living Oracle: Wisdom & Divination for Everyday Life*. *The Living Oracle* seeks to respond to this quest for divine connection and guidance, as pervasive in the new Millennium (in our own era) as it has been throughout human history. Indeed, *The Living Oracle* strives, unabashedly, to introduce to a wider readership a practical, contemporary experience in oracular consultation. Those already familiar with the use of oracles are invited to let themselves be "informed" by yet another manifesta-

---

[1] The *I Ching* has its origins in ancient China (Shang Dynasty, early second millennium B.C.E.); the Tarot was reportedly introduced into France in the late fourteenth century, A.C.E., with possible Indian origins far earlier; the Runes is of Viking/Teutonic origins (ca. third century B.C.E.)

tion of oracular consciousness—one probably quite different from anything previously experienced. Those new to oracular consultation are invited to make their own exciting discoveries as to just how pertinent, relevant and timely, in our own day, this ancient tradition's methods for attaining to wisdom and guidance can be.

To this end, *The Living Oracle: Wisdom & Divination for Everyday Life* is an eager and willing volume created to relate to you in consistently helpful ways. By design it is portable enough to accompany you on life's journey, standing at the ready to lend surer guidance and safer passage through the rigors of daily travail, challenges and triumphs.

The Living Oracle consists of sixty-four slices of Universe. Each "slice" is a written passage consisting of a "wisdom" portion and a "divination" portion. However, you, the reader and consulter, should bear in mind that, in keeping with the spirit of such long-standing oracles as the aforementioned *I Ching*, Tarot and Runes, the wisdom and divination associated with this volume are not, per se, what is contained in these passages. Rather, wisdom and divination arise primarily from the interaction—even the dialectic—that spontaneously transpire in your mind in relation to the written material in the course of a reading or consultation. The readings offered here are presented in such a way as to be sufficiently evocative to draw forth the wisdom and divination which are inherent within each and every one of us.

I make no particular claim to being either uniquely wise or clairvoyant. My function in *The Living Oracle's* coming to be has been more in serving as "midwife," and scribe, to the process, channeling and recording the material for the oracular passages as it was passed through me over the course of many months, and then subsequently writing the orienting chapters over the following three years or so. All of the first-draft writing was done longhand, and much of it was done outdoors, either while sitting beneath my favorite "meditation tree" in Cambridge, Massachusetts, or looking out over the Gulf of Saint Lawrence from Mabou, Cape Breton Island, Nova Scotia, or in my hideaway by the banks of the Deerfield River in Western Massachusetts. Much of the editing took place either in my little room in Conantum (Emerson & Thoreau country), in Concord, Massachusetts, or in my study, located at the end of a labyrinthine series of corridors and stairways in a church in Newton, Massachusetts. It just seemed that this book really wanted to be written, and it wrote itself. It is my earnest hope that my psyche has become, through well over a half century of current embodied life, enough of a crucible to have stewed up compilations of material of suitable scope to evoke or engage you, the reader. The intention, throughout, has been one of providing an avenue of true assistance to you.

As an additional note of possible interest, I would acknowledge simply that I have been a student of schools of wisdom and divinatory methods and a practitioner of meditation for well over a quarter of a century, and that prior to, and during, the writing of this book I had been, and was, electively living a solitary and celibate life over a considerable period of time.

All good oracles have a "living" energy about them. They are alive. They come to life to do what they do through the very act of being consulted. As you come to participate in the life of this oracle, please know that the wisdom and divination that will arise for you in the course of consulting *The Living Oracle* are truly yours. Such wisdom and guidance may arise amidst your reactions to the various passages that are either consonant, dissonant, or both. That is, you need only discover *some* vantage point—some flow of response—whatever it may be, in the course of consulting, reflecting upon, and freely associating with the material, to have wisdom and divination emerge during a consultation.

I therefore commend to you, with pleasure, *The Living Oracle: Wisdom & Divination for Everyday Life.* May it find its niche amongst humankind, and live out its destiny as a *living* oracle. May it prove itself useful as staunch ally and able servant to all those who seek the wisdom of life's underlying patterns, and the divination born of the experience of universal interconnectedness. May you find through your interactions with it a source of true inspiration and guidance, an ongoing contemporary experience of personal, Divine connection, and a surer sense of living within a context of Grace in which human experience is lovingly held as divinely meaningful.

Yours, with love on our shared journey,

Stephen Rich Merriman

Shelburne Falls, Massachusetts
USA
February 27th, 2002

On Consulting the Oracle

The act of consulting *The Living Oracle* is really an adventure in "serious play." The serious part has to do with making the choice to deal, consciously, with those dramas that adorn our everyday life. All of us, without exception, are obliged to experience a wide range of heartbreaks and joys, successes and failures, realized hopes and dreams dashed. Life seems, at times, to be a rather constant array of challenges in which we both win and lose (perhaps depending upon the day!). So, yes, there is this serious side to things—no mistaking that.

But then again, there is the "play" side. If tiptoeing through a minefield by moonlight is daunting, the experience of finding ourselves in the midst of often quirky, half-fathomed, silvery-lit "suddennesses" can be magical. In fact, consulting oracles is *fun*, and it's O.K. that it is! So the playful part of all this has everything to do with the sense of adventure and engagement which arise through the inquiries, rituals and readings themselves. One often senses, in the course of a consultation, a shifting of one's being and consciousness into greater alignment with the harmony in which the Universe ultimately holds us, and one starts to absorb this sense of larger connectedness amidst tissues of revealed meaning. These are *felt* senses, and as they become incorporated into our being they become companionable to us, bringing out humorous and off-beat facets of our personalities just as readily as they may reveal more dark and serious sides. Whether one experiences life as basically a tragedy punctuated, at times, by comic relief, or whether life seems, rather, primarily comical or absurd, as colored by passing interludes of deep drama, probably depends on the temperament of the individual. The *Oracle*, however, speaks to both possibilities as co-operative, and the "playful" does not necessarily get upstaged by the "serious." Perhaps Dante truly got it right when he entitled his magnum opus *The Divine Comedy*.

Formulating an inquiry

To consult *The Living Oracle*, it is usually necessary to approach it with a question, or inquiry, in mind. The process of forming an inquiry is important: inquiries need to be given some degree of serious consideration. Although *The Living Oracle* does not require that you bare your innermost heart in the questions you pose to it (although should you choose to bare your innermost heart, *The Living Oracle* will strive to respond accordingly), inquiries need to be about events, people, places, things, situations, circumstances, institutions, environments, viewpoints, or ideas that matter to you. Often it is useful to reflect for several moments (or longer) about what to pose to it, so that, in gathering your thoughts, a certain refinement in the nature of framing the inquiry can occur.

Then, once the wording of the inquiry comes to you, you may want to write it down, date it and sign it. These actions establish your inquiry as a "matter of record" within the Cosmos, and are an apt ritual. Whatever sense of dignity (or frivolity) that you bring to the process will be reflected in the nature of the responses received. Your own rituals regarding consulting *The Living Oracle* will likely take on a more personal aspect over time, and these inclinations are a part of your growing relationship with the *Oracle*, and can be trusted.

Easy consultation methods

Once an inquiry is formulated, there is really no incorrect method for consulting *The Living Oracle*. For instance, you can, if you wish, mentally formulate an inquiry, and then open the book at random with eyes closed, letting a finger fall to the page. This is probably the simplest and most immediate method.

Another method is to use *The Living Oracle* as a reader, perhaps consulting the listing of passages in the table of contents, with the intention of letting your attention be drawn to one or more of the Passage headings which appear to have a bearing on your situation at the moment of inquiry. In fact, if you're not sure *what* you're feeling at the moment, just scanning the Passage headings in the table of contents can help place you in touch with *something* that's going on inside you. Certain passage headings will likely strike a resonance within you—jump out at you—and you can proceed from there to the specific passages themselves, confident that you are getting in touch with some aspect of your being, once again. Such impromptu methods can yield very satisfying results, and you are, or course, free to develop your own variations, as need and intuition may dictate.

The coin methods

The methods that follow are foreseen as likely being the most frequently used ones for consulting *The Living Oracle* as an oracle. They are a bit more formal, require a little more work, but are very effective. The first method involves the use of a coin, which is tossed, or cast, six times. After formulating a question or inquiry, the coin is tossed, and the heads and tails of each cast is recorded horizontally, forming a sequence of H's and T's, as in THHHTH. Compare this sequence to the Table of Sequences on p. 173 (also on the back cover) to find the appropriate passage that comes forth, thereby, in response to your inquiry.

For those of you who want to learn more about the mathematics involved in the process of selection during the coin tosses of a single sequence, this information is presented in some detail in the appendix on p. 179.

Combination readings

Combination readings involving two or more passages may be constructed to good effect. Additionally, it needs to be noted that combinations involving three or more passages can become quite voluminous in terms of elicited material. If one sets time aside (almost as in a mini-retreat), carefully formulates an inquiry and sets up a combination, such an experience can easily be the equivalent of an hour or more of intensive psychotherapy. *The Living Oracle* can (and indeed is designed to) render this kind of interaction. If, on the other hand, an inquiry needs to be made on the fly (and for other kinds of brief inquiries, as well), consultation based on a single passage or a shorter combination of passages may be preferable.

The "two-passage" reading

A two-passage combination is comprehensive enough to cover many contingencies. This involves forming an inquiry, and then, using the coin method, eliciting two passages. *Headings*—categories of response—are assigned for each passage of the combination. In a two-passage combination the headings to which each passage constitutes a response are the *Current Situation (Overview)*, and the *Evolved Situation (Outcome)*, respectively.

Having formed an inquiry, a two-passage combination can be arrived at in two ways. The first way is to simply cast a single coin in two groupings of six tosses each, and then record the passage unearthed by the first six casts—the *Current Situation (Overview)* passage—and then by the second six casts—the *Evolved Situation (Outcome)* passage.

The second way to arrive at a two-passage combination is to simultaneously throw two coins of different denominations, say a penny and a nickel, for example. Decide ahead of time which coin will be used to supply the heads and tails sequence for the *Current Situation (Overview)* and *Evolved Situation (Outcome)*, respectively; it doesn't matter which is which, but once you choose, you must be consistent.

The two coins are then cast together six times. The sequence of heads and tails for each coin is recorded separately. In this example, if you've decided that the penny is to provide the sequence for the *Current Situation*

(Overview) part of the *Oracle's* response, then the passage derived from the penny's sequence of heads and tails is the *Current Situation (Overview)* response, while the passage derived from the nickel's sequence of heads and tails is the *Evolved Situation (Outcome)* response.

More advanced consultation methods

The three-passage combination can also be easily used in consulting *The Living Oracle*. This combination is my personal favorite, and more advanced readings (to be described presently) are built upon it. The passage headings employed in this combination are *Current Situation (Overview), Forthcoming Influences (Developments),* and *Evolved Situation (Outcome).*

To proceed with a consultation based on three passages, formulate your inquiry, and then use three coins of different denominations (perhaps, say, a penny, a nickel, and a dime, respectively for each of the response headings). Decide which coin will supply the sequence for the passage addressing each portion of the *Oracle's* response (*Current Situation [Overview], Forthcoming Influences [Developments]* and *Evolved Situation [Outcome],* respectively). Then, again being consistent, cast the three coins as a group six times, record each coin's own sequence of heads and tails as distinct from the others. The penny sequence, for instance, can ferret out the *Current Situation (Overview)* passage, the nickel sequence can be used to arrive at the *Forthcoming Influences (Developments)* passage, and the dime sequence can be used to designate the *Evolved Situation (Outcome)* passage.

From "three" to "four or five"

Thus far, a reading arising from this method of consultation gives you a lot of information. This reading, however, can yet be deepened in immense ways. These ways include both the unlocking of up to two additional (highly) *Relevant Passages* from the *The Living Oracle* text, and the establishing of cross-correspondence to passages and commentary relating directly to pertinent *I Ching* hexagrams and their "changing lines" (if any).[1]

First, here is how to access up to two highly *Relevant Passages* already encoded in the matrix of your three-passage consultation:

In any three-passage consultation, it is theoretically possible to have a line-up of any combination of the 64 passages, including both "twins" and "triplets" of the same passage. However, as just mentioned, encoded within the methodology for obtaining the first three passages is the option to derive up to two additional passages, the *Relevant Passages*, from the first three. I would note here that *Relevant Passages* can have an importance to an overall consultation equal in significance to the first three passages.[2]

To demonstrate how to unlock up to two additional passages that bear particular relevance to the consultation at hand, I shall arbitrarily select three combinations (and therefore passages). Pretend for a moment that we've formed our inquiry, simultaneously cast a penny, a nickel and a dime six times, recorded their sequences, and, via consulting the Table of Sequences[3], come up with the following combos:

---

[1] Within any specific consultation of *The Living Oracle*, there may or may not be changing lines in corresponding *I Ching* hexagrams. This is is encoded in the pattern of sequences rendered in the process of evoking a response from *The Living Oracle*, which is subsequently explained in great detail.

[2] For additional perspective on the matter, please consult "The relevance of the *Relevant Passages*" on p. 29.

[3] The number and name of the specific passage that each combination refers to can be found by consulting the Table of Sequences (p. 173 or on the back cover of this book).

Current Situation (Overview)

TTHHTH

#51 Compassion

Forthcoming Influences

THTHHT

#42 Mystery

Evolved Situation (Outcome)

THTHTH

#43 Patience

Thus far we have the three combinations (one for each denomination of coin) arrayed horizontally, each of which, in this example, references to Passage 51, 42, and 43, respectively. However we also have six columns of three characters each arrayed *vertically*. Each vertical column, in this example, consists of a three member series of heads and tails, as follows:

Current Situation (Overview)	T	T	H	H	T	H
Forthcoming Influences	T	H	T	H	H	T
Evolved Situation (Outcome)	T	H	T	H	T	H

We can now proceed to combine each of the *vertical* columns, using the following guidelines:

3 T's	2 T's & 1 H	2 H's & 1 T	3 H's
↓	↓	↓	↓
<u>T</u>	H	T	<u>H</u>

So following these guidelines, we can take the vertical columns that resulted from our horizontal combinations (from the simultaneous castings of the penny, nickel and dime) and combine them:

Current Situation (Overview)	T	T	H	H	T	H
Forthcoming Influences	T	H	T	H	H	T
Evolved Situation (Outcome)	T	H	T	H	T	H
	$\underline{I}$	T	H	$\underline{H}$	H	T

Therefore, in accordance with these directions, the 1st Relevant Passage to emerge from our three horizontal sequences is:

1st Relevant Passage $\underline{I}$TH$\underline{H}$HT   #50 PERDITION

By now you have probably noticed that combining three H's or three T's vertically results not in T or H, but in $\underline{I}$ or $\underline{H}$, respectively.

What is the significance of $\underline{I}$ and $\underline{H}$ you ask?

First of all, there is no significance to a $\underline{I}$ or an $\underline{H}$ for the *1st Relevant Passage*; the *1st Relevant Passage*; is simply whatever the combination of H's and T's is, regardless of any underlined $\underline{H}$'s or $\underline{I}$'s. However, we derive the *2nd Relevant Passage* from the first by converting $\underline{H}$'s to T's and $\underline{I}$'s to H's.

And so:

Our *1st Relevant Passage #50* ($\underline{I}$TH$\underline{H}$HT), derived from the first three passages, changes, or transforms, into:

2nd Relevant Passage   HTHTHT   #22 INNOCENCE

Hence, the complete series of readings, based in this instance on our hypothetical (and, in this example, unspecified) inquiry is:

Current Situation	T	T	H	H	T	H	#51 COMPASSION
Forthcoming Influences	T	H	T	H	H	T	#42 MYSTERY
Evolved Situation	T	H	T	H	T	H	#43 PATIENCE
1st Relevant Passage	I	T	H	H	H	T	#50 PERDITION
2nd Relevant Passage	H	T	H	T	H	T	#22 INNOCENCE

In practice you're likely to discover that a four- or five-passage consultation elicits as much material, within a given sitting, as can reasonably be digested for quite a while thereafter. Such a thorough consultation, drawing on the *Oracle* to provide its fullest response, can be very intense, and very helpful. The reader/consulter should feel free to devise other methods of consultation as intuition may warrant.

> *If combining the vertical columns yields only H's or T's, and no H's or I's, then only one Relevant Passage is derived from the first three combinations, and the entire reading is a "four-passage" reading.*

Connectivity to, and correspondence with, the *I Ching*

For those of you who wish, as yet, to further deepen and enrich a consultation, and are developing, or already have, a familiarity with (and undoubtedly an affinity to) the *I Ching, or Book of Changes* (I favor the Wilhelm/Baynes edition[4], but any *I Ching* edition that appeals to you will also work

---

[4] Grateful acknowledgement is made to Princeton University Press for permission to quote extensively from the Wilhelm/Baynes edition of the *I Ching* in *The Living Oracle*. For a full bibliographical citation please consult the "List of Selected Readings" on p. 187.

well), *The Living Oracle* offers a very rich series of correspondences with the *I Ching*, stemming directly from the *1st* and *2nd Relevant Passages*.

Here is how these correspondences are revealed:

Taking our hypothetical consultation above as a model, we can then translate each of the *Relevant Passages* into *I Ching* hexagrams. Here is how this is done:

In our current example, the *1st Relevant Passage* is:

1st Relevant Passage   I̲THH̲HT   #50 Perdition

We take the horizontal sequence of H's and I̲'s for this passage and we arrange them vertically, as shown below:

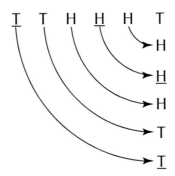

Now that the sequence of the *1st Relevant Passage* is arrayed vertically, we assign each of (H, T, H̲, I̲) a number from 6 to 9; each number then corresponds to an *I Ching* line as shown on the next page:

H̲	→ 9 →	—O—
T	→ 8 →	— —
H	→ 7 →	———
I̲	→ 6 →	—X—

Following our rules for translating each sum into an *I Ching* hexagram line we come up with (reading from bottom to top):

T	→ 8 →	— —
H	→ 7 →	———
H̲	→ 9 →	—O—
H	→ 7 →	———
T	→ 8 →	— —
I̲	→ 6 →	—X—

The resulting hexagram equates to the *I Ching* hexagram #31 *Hsien*/Influence (Wooing).

In this example, the 6 at the beginning (the bottom[5]) of the hexagram and the 9 in the fourth place are *changing lines,* and so a second hexagram is constructed from the first using the rule that 6 → 7 and 9 → 8, as shown on the next page:

---

[5] *I Ching* hexagrams are always considered to be configured from bottom to top.

First Hexagram		Second Hexagram
8 —— ——	remains	8 —— ——
7 ———————	remains	7 ———————
9 ——O——	→	8 —— ——
7 ———————	remains	7 ———————
8 —— ——	remains	8 —— ——
6 ——X——	→	7 ———————

The second hexagram equates to the *I Ching* hexagram #63 *Chi Chi*/After Completion.[6]

In subsequently consulting *I Ching* passages, one would read, in this instance, the passages pertaining to #31 *Hsien*/Influence (Wooing), and the subsequent passage designated for each of the changing lines within this hexagram—in this example the 6 at the bottom and the 9 in the fourth place (bearing in mind, once again, that *I Ching* hexagrams are always counted from the bottom up)—and then go on to consult the *I Ching* readings for hexagram #63 *Chi Chi*/After Completion.

> In its derivation and arrangement this second hexagram corresponds exactly with the sequence of our 2nd Relevant Passage from *The Living Oracle*: #22 INNOCENCE *(HTHTHT)*.

So the complete set of readings emerging from our hypothetical consultation are as follows:

---

[6] In its derivation and arrangement this second hexagram corresponds exactly with the sequence of our *2nd Relevant Passage* from *The Living Oracle*: #22 INNOCENCE *(HTHTHT)*.

From The Living Oracle

Current Situation	#51 COMPASSION
Forthcoming Influences	#42 MYSTERY
Evolved Situation	#43 PATIENCE
1st Relevant Passage	#50 PERDITION
2nd Relevant Passage	#22 INNOCENCE

Plus I Ching Correspondences

1st Relevant Passage	#31 *Hsien*/Influence (Wooing) (6 bottom, 9 fourth place)
2nd Relevant Passage	#63 *Chi Chi* /After Completion

Concerning The Living Oracle and the I Ching

In concluding this section regarding the correspondences that exist between *The Living Oracle* and the *I Ching*, I would simply mention that, with the possible exception of the actual number of passages mid-wived (which could be seen as contributing to the possibility that correspondences would emerge between the two texts), none of the correspondences, such as they are or may be, were premeditated or in any way worked out ahead of time. *The Living Oracle* text was preserved in the order in which the topics, and their respective passages, revealed themselves. In other words, there was no rearrangement of the order of passages to fit some preconceived, or subsequently conceived, schema (and no intentional working out of the original order of them, either). Similarly, the method(s) for consultation were originally envisioned as pertaining exclusively to the *The Living Oracle* text, without, initially, the notion that correspondences might exist with passages from the

I Ching. In view of all this, I feel secure in asserting that such correspondences as exist between the *1st* and *2nd Relevant Passages*, within any given consultation of *The Living Oracle*, and *I Ching* passages are synchronicitous and, in the spirit of all good oracles, all the more meaningful for that. (Please consult the following chapter, "Why *Oracles* Work," for further elucidation of this point.)

Also, I would further mention that the specific methodology by which correspondences can be sought out between *The Living Oracle* and the *I Ching* emerged quite a while after the *The Living Oracle*'s passage texts had been completed. It may be wise, in this regard, to briefly ponder certain meanings inhering in the word "correspondence." Rather than merely denoting "This equates with that," or "This goes along with that," the word "correspondence" can also be construed as implying a "flowing back and forth" between two things. Correspondence, in this sense, is not suitably designated by an equal sign, but rather by a bi-directional arrow—a "back and forth"—an exchange, of sorts. In keeping with this notion of a mutually enriching "correspondence," no passage in *The Living Oracle* was designed to "correspond to" any particular passage in the *I Ching*. However, any or all readings derived from *The Living Oracle* may, within any given moment, "correspond with" any or all passages in the *I Ching*, and vice versa. The extent and range of these apparently happenstance correspondences have yet to be fully explored, but it is hoped that a treasure trove of spurred consciousness may await discovery there.

Some additional thoughts on consulting *The Living Oracle*

Sometimes it can be wonderful to work with a close friend or confidante, perhaps taking turns making consultations of *The Living Oracle*, and then being on hand for each other to lend support and counsel as each of you reconnoiters the passages that emerge. While not taking the place of your own interaction with the *Oracle*, the input and support of friends can be of great assistance, and very reassuring. Bear in mind that any responses to your inquiry that emerge still belong to you, and whatever sense, wisdom and divination come through to you during such a consultation are between you and the *Oracle*.

One further note on the use of divinatory oracles: Overuse of them can lead to an apparent downgrading of the quality of information they yield (although this apparent downgrading may be due less to the actual pertinence of the passages evoked, and more to the limits imposed on the processing power of embodied human consciousness by neurological factors that effectively curtail the assimilation of more than a finite amount of information at any given time).

Also, regardless of whether you're skipping across the crests of waves of meaningful responses, or muddling through heaps of maddeningly cryptic belches of ambiguity, inexactitude and uncertainty, it's worthwhile remembering that, in either case, oracles are not panaceas. At their best they place you within a context of an unfolding destiny, and they point to a certain range of likelihoods, probabilities and possibilities relating to the inquiry at hand. But they cannot live your life for you. This remains your task. Within a range of likelihoods, probabilities and possibilities, options must be explored, and decisions must be made and lived out. *Only you can do this.* To recognize the necessity of personal choice, and to seek to inform each major turn in the road that is before you with a perspective of wisdom and divination—these are the correct motivations for the use of any oracle, including *The Living Oracle*. While you may not always like what it is in life that you are obliged to face and go through, you may come to experience a deeper sense of self-love regarding how you face and go through things. And, of course, life has, ineffably encoded within it, a serendipitous array of good fortune and remarkable, unanticipated blessings that also await you.

Over time you are likely to find that *The Living Oracle* will come to occupy a special place in your life and heart, not unlike the way one feels about a trusted friend who sees us through all the ups and downs that life is. Don't be too surprised if feelings of warmth and a sense of wonderful familiarity start to arise, over time, within the relationship. It is truly the richness of your unfolding relationship with your own deeper being that you are experiencing.

In closing, I wish you well as you go forward to explore and develop your relationship with *The Living Oracle*. In a spirit of "serious play," may you and *The Living Oracle* go on to share many stirring adventures together!

Oracular Theory:
Why Oracles Work

The most remarkable quality about any of the "consulting" oracles—*The Living Oracle*, the Tarot, the *I Ching*, the Runes (as well as so many others)—is reflected in the notion that the invoking of a "chance" occurrence, whether this be the flip of a coin, the selection of a card, the drawing of a ceramic tablet out of a bag, can have relevance to a posed question, and connect the inquirer meaningfully to a passage or image that has a high degree of pertinence to the matter at hand. Everyday logic, which rests its case on the presumption of the linearity of cause and effect, balks at any such notion.

Even if passages arrived at seemingly by pure chance have relevance to an inquiry, one avenue to debunking oracles is to see all such texts as being written in such a vague yet inclusive way that something in all of them is bound to pertain to something that the consulter is going through, regardless of what and when that may be.

Yet the crux of the matter may hinge not so much on the apparent accuracy or aptness of a given passage, but on the resonance which the act of consulting an Oracle sets up in the person who is consulting it. Something, often utterly unexpected, is awakened, something is felt, and the interaction can be as real and compelling—and sometimes as startling—as any number of interactions between people, including those in which two people meet, unexpectedly, and discover an unanticipated "awakened" connection between them.

If we entertain, even just as a provisional hypothesis, the perennial mystical intuitions: "All is One," and "The macrocosm is contained within the microcosm" (and vice-versa), we may have a starting point to speculate about (and hopefully develop some comprehension about) oracular doings. Such mystical notions have received powerful, if largely (in terms of philosophical implications) disregarded, substantiation at the sub-atomic level through the rigorous scientific observations of particle physics and quantum mechanics, and within our own, everyday dimensional range as evidenced by the documenting of synchronicitous events, and research into the phenomenon sometimes referred to as "nonlocality."

In quantum mechanics, within certain equations describing the creation and expiration of a range of sub-atomic particles, the vectors depicting the "time" dimension have long been known to be bi-directional. Additionally, quantum mechanics has demonstrated that experimental outcomes do not exist independent of the consciousness of the observer. The consciousness of the observer is an inseparable part of the equation describing the process and outcome of such experiments; the act of observing influences (and even determines) outcome. Regarding the description of meaningful, coincidental events on the human scale, the Swiss psychiatrist C. G. Jung felt compelled to postulate the existence of an "acausal connecting principle" based on his observations of the workings of "coincidence" within his own interior (mental life) and exterior (outer world) experiences, as well as those of his patients. His monograph *Synchronicity: An Acausal Connecting Principle* remains a pioneering, seminal work in describing the arena of what is sometimes termed nonlocality. (Dr. Jung later wrote the "Foreword" to the classic Wilhelm/Baynes edition of the *I Ching*, in which he expresses his views on the acausality of oracular consultation.) In a more contemporary vein, nonlocality effects have been quantified in the work of Larry Dossey, M.D., who has studied the efficacy of prayer-at-a-distance.[7]

---

[7] Please consult the "List of Selected Readings" on page 187.

The inference that may be drawn from such concepts as quantum mechanics, synchronicity and nonlocality is that there is a domain of our being which "exists"—and functions—outside the apparent, consensually assumed limits of space and time. Within the apparently functional domain of this extended side of our being, the boundaries partitioning off the dimensions of space and time collapse, or are at least relativized to such an extent as to be momentarily suspended. This domain beyond our four-dimensional space-time perception is the domain of simultaneity in which every "thing" is connected, seamlessly, with "everything else." Stanford University neurosurgeon Karl Pribram developed the concept of the "holographic paradigm" to describe this process in which everything is simultaneously encoded within everything, and David Bohm, the late English physicist, coined the expression "implicate order" to designate this non-spatially-confined/non-temporally-confined substrate in which all phenomena, including space and time, are embedded.[8]

By tentatively positing this principle of the simultaneity of universal interconnectedness, we can begin to appreciate that the moment-of-chance which steers us to a passage in the *Oracle* is as linked to the question we pose as it is to the moment-in-time in which we pose it and even our very intention to pose it. In formulating an inquiry we upholster a "moment" in space-time with our conundrum, and then invite the nonlocality—the implicateness of the moment—to touch through simultaneity the "all-that-is," in order to gather from its interface with the implicate order that which synchronicitously pertains to our space-time situation.[9] "Chance," then, is the expression of implicateness in direct relation to the question we pose. It is the

---

[8] Please consult the "List of Selected Readings" on page 187.

[9] The syntactical awkwardnesses of several of the sentences in this paragraph are intentional. They constitute the author's attempt to render an impression, through language, of the multidimensional workings of simultaneity in the course of making an inquiry to the *Oracle*. Written, discursive language does not lend itself all that wonderfully to this task.

direct highway leading into implicateness, and back out again. At the crucial moment of "chance," the mind of the inquirer, the intention to inquire, the inquiry itself, the moment of inquiry, and the Universe's resources in addressing our inquiry (limited only by the vehicle of the *Oracle* itself and the local consciousness of the consulter)—all are "one." We are letting the interrelated pieces of an underlying, multidimensional oneness, or unity, express themselves through that very oneness at the moment of inquiry.

So it is that oracles, in partnership with our own inquiring mind, link up to, tap, and interpret, the wellspring of the beyond-linear and beyond-rational that undergirds everything we know, and can know.

A related, though decidedly more traditional, psychological way of considering the workings of oracles is to envision them as forming a channel, or pathway, external to us (our resident ego-consciousness), through which our unconscious mind can speak to, or reach, us. In this more psychological view of oracles the relevance of acausality —the non-linearity of cause and effect—still provides a starting point for comprehension. It is, however, the *source* of that which is qualified—as stemming from the unconscious mind of the person framing the inquiry, rather than from the "Universe" itself. (This may be only a specious distinction.) The psychological view holds that in our everyday state of wakeful consciousness we are often constrained against— even marshaled against—letting portions of our being reach us, especially those portions which may contain information we would rather not know or consider. To this end oracles can form a feedback loop which, as partially "external" to us and our censoring agenda, permits aspects of our unconscious to "end run" around our conscious vigilance, delusion or denial—and reach us (become known to us within our own ego-consciousness).

This view of oracles holds particular relevance to those inquiries that are responded to by seemingly "off-the-wall" passages. It can be contended that the surfacing of whatever the unconscious material is that would be perceived as posing a challenge of some kind to our conscious orientation is consistent with the evocation of strange, recondite, arcane or otherwise spurious responses via the *Oracle*. Therefore, when such a response is tendered, it is wise to not simply "shake it off like a bad pitch," but to follow wherever our mental associations and reflection, as spurred by such a passage, truly lead. In short, the extent to which a given passage strikes us as discordant to a particular inquiry may be the very extent to which that part of ourselves which is hidden from us is emerging, and finding us. In such a circumstance, the meanings encoded in particular responses may or may not seem "obvious," in addressing whatever inquiry has been made; however, the less "obvious" such meanings, at first glance, appear, the more interesting and far-reaching they may turn out to be.

Since any oracle such as the *I Ching*, the Runes, the Tarot, or *The Living Oracle* involves, in its construction, the artificial "segmentation" of the Universe into pieces through which it can subsequently speak, it should be clear that any oracle, so constructed, will "work"—the differences between various oracles being the nature of the spectrum into which the Universe is split. With any of the well-established oracles, depending on the text involved (and many oracles have numerous texts and commentaries that can be consulted), we typically find that various texts, regardless of the specific oracle to which they attach, fall along a continuum between polarities. At one end of the spectrum are texts which strive to be quite exact and cut-and-dried, in their content—not lending themselves particularly well to associative interactions on the part of the consulter. Within such texts, the potential for associative richness gets sacrificed in service of obtaining specific, declarative responses. In consulting them, one has the experience of being "told," or informed about, something—as if the provenance of the information is outside of oneself.

On the other end of the spectrum are texts which are quite vague on specifics, yet revel in a kind of imagery that leads to dynamic interactions between the passages and the consulter. Strong associative linkage is catalyzed in the process of consulting them. The experience in using such texts is that one discovers, or happens upon, responses as they arise, spontaneously, from "within." They come across as being sourced within one's own consciousness, rather than as being introduced as foreign, or external to oneself. *The Living Oracle*'s texts appear to strike a balance between offering fairly specific responses, yet retaining a kind of studied imprecision and sometimes cryptic ambiguity that can lead to strong associative linkage. This form of oracle seeks to be more engaging of the consulter than simply providing declarative "fortune telling." What "arises" is as important (if not more so) than what is "declared." As with any good oracle, any given passage can, and should, hold very different meanings depending on the nature of the inquiry to which it is in response.

Hopefully this little chapter gives you enough of a sense of grounding in oracular theory that you can make room in your life for *The Living Oracle* (as well as other oracles, should you so choose) to begin to work for you. A good oracle becomes a good friend—one who knows you really well and who can say truly wonderful things about you, as well as the difficult things that sometimes need to be said, in ways that are measured enough to be helpful, while still giving evidence of an underlying care and concern in such a manner that the motive of the counsel as "being for you own good" is never in question. Such a friend—companion—is, indeed, a rare and precious gift.

Test Inquiry: The Oracle Speaks! (...about itself...)

Regardless of pretensions—or any declared lack thereof—any oracle is only as good as its utility. There is nothing "chiseled" about an oracle's wisdom—nothing "set apart," or pedestaled. It is only in the act of being approached with an inquiry, in the experience of responding to an inquiry, and within the subsequent dialectic between the consulter and the oracle itself, and then the further assimilation and application of that experience by the consulter, that an oracle proves itself either to be worthwhile, on the one hand, or hopelessly enigmatic, spurious or otherwise a waste of time, on the other.

After the passages of *The Living Oracle* had assembled, and the methodology for consultation subsequently emerged, I used the *Oracle* quite a bit, from time to time, over the course of several years, and was often impressed with its scope and impact. A number of others used it also, not infrequently with startling and catalytic results. Many requests for the manuscript were received. Nevertheless, I knew that the one remaining chapter to be written for inclusion in the overall text was one in which *The Living Oracle* would be "put on the spot," so to speak—to reveal and declare itself, unvarnished and unadorned, to its potential readers (to those to whom it would presume to be of assistance) and let itself be heard, and examined—without any additional editing by its scribe of either the inquiry or the responses.

With all this in mind, a decision was made to pose a direct inquiry to *The Living Oracle*, dutifully recording without alteration or abridgment both the inquiry, and the *Oracle's* responses tendered to this inquiry. In truth, there was some reluctance, on my part, to do this, due to my residual apprehensions that *The Living Oracle* might serve up something ungainly or "off the wall," which could prove embarrassing to the enterprise, and undermine the *Oracle*'s perceived utility. As the vehicle who had midwived the text several years earlier, I clearly had some investment (not necessarily commendable) in the "child's" "giving a good account of itself," and I also knew that I absolutely could not dicker with whatever the *Oracle*'s responses might be, for that would be tantamount to fostering a fraudulent foundation for the *Oracle*'s credibility, and constitute a very serious breach of faith to *The Living Oracle*'s readers and consulters, as well as an affront to all that I hold dear about oracles generally. I also knew that, if I were ever stupid enough to do something like that, I would incur a heavy Karmic burden as a consequence. No thanks.

Still, I deferred for quite a while on this "chapter challenge" to *The Living Oracle*—almost three years, in fact—during which (obviously) this chapter remained unwritten, and I was laboring along with other writing projects. Nevertheless, the fact that the overall text was simply not complete without this chapter—this trial—finally got to me, and I resolved to make the inquiry.

Then, all in a moment, it became time, and I did it.

The inquiry took place in my study, hidden away at the end of a meandering course of stairways and hallways in a church in Newton, Massachusetts on Tuesday, August 1st, 2000 at about 4:30 p.m., EDT.

> Dear Living Oracle,
>
> To what purpose and destiny do you aspire—
> do you foresee for yourself?
>
> Thank you (in advance) for your response,
>
> Stephen

Please note: I forthrightly admit that this inquiry has an ambiguity to it, and to that extent this inquiry, including the wording, is sloppy. Obviously, there is a potentially crucial distinction to be made between that to which one aspires, and that which one foresees for oneself. Notwithstanding this difficulty, this *is* what was posed to *The Living Oracle*. The wording of the inquiry (unanticipated), once I was seated on the floor and open to the task, came to me quite readily, and the feeling tone around this inquiry was appropriately solemn and respectful as would befit any inquiry of serious intent.

Here is the record of *The Living Oracle's responses:*

Current Situation	T	H	H	H	H	T	#34 CELIBACY
Forthcoming Influences	T	H	H	T	T	T	#40 POLARITY
Evolved Situation	T	H	H	H	T	T	#36 VOCATION
1st Relevant Passage	I	H	H	T	H	I	#38 KINDNESS
2nd Relevant Passage	H	T	T	T	H	H	#29 ATTACHMENT

And the I Ching correspondences:

6 —X—	7 ———
7 ———	7 ———
8 — —	8 — —
9 —O—	8 — —
9 —O—	8 — —
6 —X—	7 ———
#48 *Ching* / The Well	#42 *I* / Increase

Interpretation of the Oracle's utterances

Any and all readers of *The Living Oracle* are welcome to peruse the *Oracle's* responses (consulting the full reading for Passages #34, #40, #36, #38, and #29, respectively), along with the *I Ching* correspondences, and to consider, within the context of the original inquiry, whether *The Living Oracle* gives a fair account of itself.

As *The Living Oracle's* midwife, I shall also venture, in print, down the path a bit in this direction, though I must hasten to add that whatever I have to contribute to the interpretation or deciphering of these passages may actually have more to do with, and reveal more about, my interpretive abilities (such as they are), than about *The Living Oracle* and its intentions. No reader is obliged to take anything I might render as to interpretation as being in any way definitive, nor as any substitute for her/his own interpretive efforts.

Here again is the inquiry, exactly as posed to the *Oracle*, followed by my interpretation of the *Oracle's* responses:

> Dear Living Oracle,
>
> To what purpose and destiny do you aspire— do you foresee for yourself?
>
> Thank you (in advance) for your response,
>
> Stephen

Current Situation (Overview)

#34 CELIBACY (ABSTINENCE) (Full text, p. 108)

One of the threads of Celibacy (Abstinence) is the notion that less is more. For instance, less indulgence leads to more refinement in perception and awareness—in consciousness. Whatever is personal, tied to, and derived from indulgence is "fractured," by celibacy, so that a whole new perception that is transpersonal can emerge. There is also the notion, in this passage, of laying "a foundation, to set an anchorage in the non-material realm in which one discovers a home base in a place and a way of life where one never thought it would be discovered." The *Oracle* seems to be noting, to its readers, its rather simple origins, at least as being channeled through a life that was pared way back—had become very plain and free of indulgence— and claim this foundation as its own. The *Oracle* also suggests that it is now capable of being befriended, and constitutes "a channel through which one's [consulters'] life priorities can explicate themselves with sometimes startling clarity." The *Oracle* maintains that, at this point, it can be trusted in bringing into the foreground the life priorities of those who would consult it and that it, the *Oracle*, claims to constitute a point of contact with "the bedrock of the Self."

Forthcoming Influences (Developments)

#40 POLARITY (Full text, p. 120)

The *Oracle* appears to take this opportunity to express its philosophical orientation, which eschews simplistic (and cheap) solutions, predictions and counsel based on one-sidedness and "black and white thinking." Whatever is to develop within the life of this *Oracle* (and perhaps within the lives of those who consult it) is apparently to have more to do with learning to live consciously within, and amidst, the tension, potential and charge of polar opposites rather than with seeking to eliminate or cast out *anything*. It appears to claim that its own consciousness—the very consciousness that comprises the *Oracle* itself—is based solidly in this state of suspension between opposing forces, and it suggests that a kind of success, for it, and presumably for its consulters, is to be found in approaching knowledge, wisdom and divination in this fashion. Perhaps *The Living Oracle* is forecasting (or at least aspires to) a continuation of its growth in consciousness as an oracle, as it pledges itself to continue to reside within, betwixt and between the very tensions of those who come to it for assistance. This very tension is what "feeds" the *Oracle*.

Evolved Situation (Outcome)

#36 VOCATION (CALLING) (Full text, p. 112)

It is curious to see what *The Living Oracle* either aspires to, or foresees for itself, in terms of its evolved situation (outcome). In either case, it comes down solidly on the side of the pragmatic. Once again, the *Oracle* cites a suspension—in this case the suspension between "the apparent meaninglessness of unfulfilling work," and "the quickening sense of purposeful activity with which the energy of calling can fill us." The *Oracle* notes, "There are always trade-offs between the exigencies of self-support and survival, on the one hand, and the soul's calling to come forth into meaningful activity, on the other."

I wonder, in going over this passage within the context of the inquiry, whether the *Oracle* is pondering (and perhaps divining) whatever the trade-offs are that will await it in the course of finding a publisher and being published or disseminated in some fashion—an exigency of self-support and survival, to be sure—but, apparently, of only questionable worth were the *Oracle* to give itself over to this cheaply by way of letting itself be "dumbed down" in pursuit of meeting some momentary "'hot market' for . . . goods and services," and the short-term "monetary gains and material comforts" that are the seductions of such a course. On the other hand, suggests the *Oracle*, if it were to be given over solely to the purity of its calling, and remain rarefied and inaccessible in the pristineness of existing as a solitary manuscript gathering dust on a shelf somewhere, it could be sacrificing equally important parts of what could be a fulfilling destiny. The *Oracle* states the desirability of balancing both considerations, and probably its intentions to do so, and, we might surmise, resolves to remain "wholly" itself, "regardless of which end of the meaningless ⟵——————⟶ meaningful continuum" it is, "within any moment, visiting."

The *Oracle* suggests that its truer vocation—and destiny—can be (will be?) realized by moving freely back and forth between both territories, disregarding neither. Perhaps there is also something in the *Oracle*'s assessment of its evolved situation, or destiny, which opines on the way its readers will use it: in a sense that it is O.K., and expected, that its destiny includes being used in pursuit of guidance and divination in both the sphere of the mundane, or practical, and the sphere of attaining to wisdom, spiritual attunement and expanded consciousness for their own sake.

The relevance of the Relevant Passages

In the first three passages are addressed *Current Situation (Overview)*, *Forthcoming Influences (Developments)*, and *Evolved situation (Outcome)*, respectively. These headings are unmistakably temporally linked; they indicate responses that speak to a progression in the time dimension. The additional *Relevant Passages*, however, need not necessarily be temporally re-lated to the first three passages. The relationship of the *Relevant Passages* to the passages that precede them (and the relationship inhering between the *Relevant Passages* themselves) may or may not appear obvious in the course of a consultation. Other possibilities that *Relevant Passages* seek to address could include "other factors to be considered," or "qualities attending to the current situation," or "actions to be avoided (or undertaken)"—or any other associative heading that occurs to the interpretive imagination in the course of a reading. Although it may seem less precise that *Relevant Passages* can occur in the absence of a nifty schema for incorporating them, it is my ex-perience that *they are of full, equal importance to the preceding temporally-linked passages in the completeness and applicability of a reading.* Their lack of obvious temporal connection does not necessarily mean that no temporal connection exists, only that their connection and relevance to the passages that precede them are not necessarily as concerned with the temporal. Hav-ing stated this qualification, I proceed to a brief exploration of that portion of the *Oracle*'s response as revealed through the *Relevant Passages*.

1st Relevant Passage

#38 KINDNESS (GOODWILL) (Full text, p. 116)

The *Oracle* seems to go to great lengths in this passage to claim kindness and goodwill as its abiding qualities (or at least this is its aspiration). These qualities are to inform all of its responses to those who would seek its divina-tion and counsel. It harbors no ill will and, if approached disrespectfully, will nevertheless "resist the vindictive impulse and find a compassionate basis" for its response. The *Oracle* announces its intention to proceed on this basis always, and, undoubtedly, counsels its readers and would-be consulters to cultivate these qualities as well. In speaking through "Kindness," the *Oracle* is trying to give reassurance of its benign intentions to all those whom it would assist.

2nd Relevant Passage

#29 ATTACHMENT (Full text, p. 98)

In this passage the *Oracle* appears to make a comment about its own existence—perhaps going out of its way to reveal that it, too, is imperfect and still growing, and perhaps even striving for levels of conscious realization that are beyond the attainable for it. Perhaps it holds itself up to us, saying, in a way, "Look at me: Despite the scope of what I know and how I function, I'm not perfect either, and can make no such representation." The *Oracle* may be pointing out that is has a relatively limited range of expression (true of all oracles), given that its representations of the "Universe" are limited to sixty-four "slices." However, notwithstanding this limitation and the imperfections within each "slice" through which it speaks, the *Oracle* recognizes that it can have no realized life without them. The *Oracle* may even be suggesting that it, indeed, functions better as an oracle through the very admission of its limitations and imperfections. To this extent it wishes us to regard it as one with us.

I Ching Correspondences

#48 Ching / The Well → #42 I / Increase

What may be truly profound—and also quite amusing—is that in seeking *I Ching* correspondences to the *Oracle*'s own pronouncements, *The Living Oracle* can be seen as soliciting input from another source, in this case another oracle (and such a venerable one at that!), regarding its own aspirations and destiny as an oracle. (Of course, this is not the only way this interaction can be construed.)

And the *I Ching* does not disappoint:

Hexagram #48 Ching / The Well

Given the context of the inquiry, this hexagram has everything to do with noting the requirements for an oracle to be effective, and the conditions of refurbishment that *The Living Oracle* is undergoing (including, perhaps, the undertaking of this very chapter), along with a prognosis. The well, as a dispenser of nourishment, is a fitting symbol for an oracle. Following the image further, the commentary (Wilhelm/Baynes edition) on this hexagram notes:

> Thus the well is the symbol of that social structure which, evolved by mankind in meeting its most primitive needs, is independent of all political forms. Political structures change, as do nations, but the life of man with its needs remains eternally the same—this cannot be changed. Life is also inexhaustible. It grows neither less nor more; it exists for one and for all. The generations come and go, and all enjoy life in its inexhaustible abundance.
>
> However, there are two prerequisites for a satisfactory political or social organization of mankind. We must go down to the very foundations of life. For any merely superficial ordering of life that leaves its deepest needs unsatisfied is as ineffectual as if no attempt at order had ever been made.

So oracles, observes the *I Ching* to *The Living Oracle*, have to be capable of "digging deep," or, rather (in keeping with the hexagram's metaphor), have to be "deeply dug," if they are to serve as worthy dispensers of nourishment.

In THE IMAGE (a text heading in *I Ching* hexagram #48), the following statement appears:

> Water over wood: the image of THE WELL.
> Thus the superior man encourages the people at their work,
> And exhorts them to help one another.

The *I Ching*, in this passage, seems to be both encouraging *The Living Oracle* as a "superior man" would encourage others, and reaffirming to *The Living Oracle* that "exhorting people to help one another" is the calling for all good oracles.

Within the changing lines of hexagram #48, the *I Ching* appears to offer clues as to the dynamic state of development pertaining to *The Living Oracle*.

In "Six at the beginning" (the bottom line of the hexagram) there is the observation (admonition?) that:

> One does not drink the mud of the well.
> No animals come to an old well.

This seems to counsel *The Living Oracle* not to fall into disrepair (and disrepute) by limiting its sphere of activity to parlor games or lower pursuits (astral level phenomena or "new age" sideshows?), nor fall into disuse. The warning, so to speak, has once again to do, at least in part, with seeking publication only through a venerable publisher, rather than a faddish, fly-by-night buck-chaser which would leave it dumbed down, seduced, rendered unrecognizable and, ultimately, abandoned. In any event, if *The Living Oracle* "throws (itself) away," it will not be sought.

In "Nine in the second place," the commentary reads, in part:

> The water itself is clear, but is not being used . . .
> This describes the situation of a person who possesses good qualities but neglects them.

The passage seems self-explanatory. It's also possible that the *I Ching* may here be noting that the *Oracle*, despite the quality of its "water," has, since the oracular passages were completed, remained on the shelf for several years, relatively ignored by its midwife, misgauged, along the way, by a few literary agents, and unrecognized as to its true value by a certain segment of the publishing industry.

In "Nine in the third place," the text goes:

> The well is cleaned, but no one drinks from it.
> This is my heart's sorrow,
> For one might draw from it.

> If the king were clear-minded,
> Good fortune might be enjoyed in common.

The commentary on the text for this line is:

> An able man is available. He is like a purified well whose water is drinkable. But no use is made of him. This is the sorrow of those who know him. One wishes that the prince might learn about it; this would be good fortune for all concerned.

This line, on balance, strikes a more hopeful tone. First, the *I Ching* reiterates that the "water" in *The Living Oracle* is good, and then goes further to express a sadness that the *Oracle* is not being used to provide nourishment. However, the *I Ching*, in this text, holds out some hope for a change in this state of affairs. Perhaps the "king" (or "prince") signifies a sympathetic and capable editor who would hold some sway over the procurement of an appropriate publishing venue for *The Living Oracle*. Then, perhaps:

> Good fortune might be enjoyed in common . . .
> This would be good fortune for all concerned.[10]

In "Six at the top," the text goes:

> One draws from the well Without hindrance. It is dependable.
> Supreme good fortune.

The commentary on this line reads:

> The well is there for all. No one is forbidden to take water from it. No matter how many come, all find what they need, for the well is dependable. It has a spring and never runs dry. Therefore it is a great blessing to the whole land. The same is true of the really great man, whose inner wealth is inexhaustible; the more that people draw from him, the greater his wealth becomes.

---

[10] As *The Living Oracle* has reached you in book form, you can be assured that this is what has come to pass.

The *I Ching*, with this changing line and its passage and commentary, seems to proclaim that *The Living Oracle*'s future/destiny is very auspicious, or at least holds out significant hope that *The Living Oracle*'s aspirations and destiny can be realized—perhaps a triumph not just for *The Living Oracle* (or the *I Ching*, which hardly needs more recognition) but a triumph, as well, for the non-rational, living substrate which undergirds the *I Ching*, *The Living Oracle* and all other good oracles. Upon reflection, it would be hard to imagine a more favorable prognosis for *The Living Oracle* than that which the *I Ching* appears to confer upon it via this changing line.

Hexagram #42 I / *Increase*

In this hexagram the *I Ching* holds out to *The Living Oracle* its own creed: "the fundamental idea on which the *Book of Changes* is based. To rule is to serve." The theme of this hexagram is "increase through sacrifice."

> A sacrifice of the higher element that produces an increase of the lower is an out-and-out increase. It indicates the spirit that alone has the power to help the world.

THE JUDGMENT of hexagram #42 reads:

> Increase. It furthers one
> To undertake something.
> It furthers one to cross the great water.

The *I Ching* appears here to be encouraging, even emboldening, *The Living Oracle* to embark on its destiny, now that its water is clear and ready to be drawn.

The *I Ching*, in the commentary on THE JUDGMENT, goes on to point out that:

> . . . in such times of progress and successful development   it is
> necessary to work and make the best use of the time. The time
> resembles that of a marriage of heaven and earth, when the earth
> partakes of the creative power of heaven, forming and bringing

forth living beings. The time of INCREASE does not endure, therefore it must be utilized while it lasts.

So, apparently, *The Living Oracle* is to ride some favorable currents through which it will find a sphere of application and usefulness that will help launch it into its work, and the realization of its destiny as a living, working oracle—*and*, the *Oracle* must use this initial auspicious period of expansion as thoroughly as possible, so that when the climate inevitably transitions into something less favorable to this kind of expansion, the *Oracle* will already have become established enough to make it through a leaner, or less auspicious, period.

The *I Ching* also appears to further counsel *The Living Oracle* on its own future development as an oracle. In the text called THE IMAGE (of hexagram #42), the *I Ching* states:

> Wind and thunder: the image of INCREASE.
> Thus the superior man:
> If he sees good, he imitates it;
> If he has faults, he rids himself of them.

The commentary on THE IMAGE points out that the path that is mentioned in THE IMAGE text constitutes an "ethical change" that "represents the most important increase in personality." Here the *I Ching* continues to encourage *The Living Oracle* to aspire to a high calling, that of striving to bring out the higher calling in all those it would serve.

Summary of *The Living Oracle's* response to the inquiry

The Living Oracle, in responding to the direct inquiry made to it regarding its aspirations and destiny, claims humble, simple origins which have opened it as a point of contact to larger consciousness, and have also opened it to being befriended (PASSAGE #34). The *Oracle* finds its identity through knowingly letting itself be in suspension between sharp, seemingly irreconcilable viewpoints and energies, without coming down with finality on one side or the other (Passage #40). It sees its vocation as dancing the tightrope between what it takes to survive, on the one hand, and yet, on the other, remain as true as it can to the purity of its calling (Passage #36). It declares its goodness and goodwill as its primary orientation towards all who would consult it (Passage #38), and it acknowledges its own imperfections and limitations, noting that its own existence and consciousness are also, unavoidably, predicated on attachment, and that its limitations are also, in part, related to having so few avenues (the Passages) through which to "speak." The *Oracle* states, however, that it may actually constitute a better *Oracle* for the presence of its imperfections and limitations, and its awareness of them (Passage #29).

The *I Ching*, through the correspondences with the *Relevant Passages*, would, at face value, appear to give recognition to the existence of a kindredness between the two oracles, and to confer a decided value and dignity on *The Living Oracle*, with its repeated references to the purity of *The Living Oracle*'s "water," and the readiness for that water to be drawn, and drawn upon. Indeed, both oracles are "wells" from which one can draw. The *I Ching* both endorses (assays?) the purity of *The Living Oracle*'s "water," and is saddened that *The Living Oracle* has not yet (as of the time of this inquiry) been recognized and utilized—but it foresees the fulfilling of a helpful and nourishing role and destiny for *The Living Oracle*, while ever encouraging it to remain true to the intention of helping others to make moral and ethical gains in their lives, and reminding it that "To rule truly is to serve."

This consultation of *The Living Oracle* about its aspirations and destiny was predicated on the need to "test" the *Oracle*. I can offer no more than to have faithfully recorded the inquiry that was placed before it, and the *Oracle*'s responses to that inquiry, as well as the *I Ching*'s correspondences with those responses, in accordance with the consulting methodology. I have also ventured to render one possible translation of what might be any number of interpretations of *The Living Oracle*'s responses.

Again, the reader (or consulter) is encouraged to form her/his own impressions of the *Oracle's* responses to this "test" inquiry and, hopefully, given some reassurance based on this, to proceed on to entering into a working relationship with *The Living Oracle*, discovering through direct encounter and experience if the *Oracle* is as it would appear to be.

The Living Oracle

#1 TRUTH	#33 GUILE
#2 LUST (CRAVING)	#34 CELIBACY (ABSTINENCE)
#3 LOVE	#35 BLISS
#4 HOPE	#36 VOCATION (CALLING)
#5 EVIL	#37 BETRAYAL
#6 GESTATION	#38 KINDNESS (GOOD WILL)
#7 VIGIL	#39 DEATH
#8 PEACE	#40 POLARITY
#9 RENEWAL	#41 GENEROSITY
#10 GRACE	#42 MYSTERY
#11 SUBLIMITY	#43 PATIENCE
#12 HATRED	#44 VANITY
#13 LOSS	#45 REALITY
#14 DELIVERANCE	#46 CONSCIOUSNESS
#15 FRIGHT / TERROR	#47 LIFE
#16 RESOLVE	#48 RESTORATION
#17 HEART	#49 REPENTANCE
#18 TRANSITION	#50 PERDITION (DAMNATION)
#19 TRANSCENDENCE	#51 COMPASSION
#20 ANGER	#52 LEGACY
#21 REJECTION	#53 CREATIVITY
#22 INNOCENCE	#54 PROVIDENCE
#23 STEWARDSHIP	#55 JUDGEMENT (ASSESSMENT)
#24 LONELINESS	#56 PROMISE (FULFILLMENT)
#25 HONESTY	#57 REBUFF
#26 REST	#58 INDIFFERENCE
#27 FREEDOM	#59 VULNERABILITY
#28 DESPAIR	#60 COMMUNITY
#29 ATTACHMENT	#61 DIGNITY
#30 NUTURANCE	#62 ELOQUENCE
#31 EMPTINESS	#63 COMPLETION (FULLNESS)
#32 ANTICIPATION	#64 THE UNKNOWABLE

THE PASSAGES

Passage #1

Truth

Wisdom

Truth is reality revealed—made conscious, set plain. And yet, all realities are relative, as are their respective truths—including this one. Hence, many solid-sounding truths are inherently self-contradictory. For instance, the apparently inalienable truth of one's love may galvanize the truth of one's hatred. Yesterday's victim is likely to be today's abuser. Is there truth in victimhood? Yes. Is there truth in the grounds for abusing? Yes. *Every* state of consciousness, from the most prosaic to the most esoteric—from the ecstasy of intoxicating indulgence to the somberness of sober abstaining—has its truth: its down-to-earth conviction of "how things are." At the level of quantum mechanics, however, truths haze out into smudges of likelihoods and probabilities. There are *many* versions of how things are; each one of which has a certain validity; each one of which likes to masquerade as truth with a capital "T." Each truth "buys its own trip," so to speak. Truth needn't be dishonored, only relativized. To search for absolute truth is like searching for absolute matter, an infinite regress of subdivisions. The same holds for the search for truth about oneself. Absolute knowledge of self is not possible. We cannot encompass the totality of self. Perhaps there are too many "totalities of self"; they slip through our net of seeking so very, very easily. We can ride the flow of who we experience ourselves to be, and, with luck, recognize some portion of truth about ourselves by the effects we create and the legacy we leave in our wake.

Divination

You may be selling out to a capital "T" truth, sparing yourself the more relevant task of taking into account the tapestry of small "t" truths operative in the situation, or (since truth is inherently self-contradictory) you may be called upon to awaken to a significant small "t" truth from a slumber of complacency. If you have swallowed a capital "T" truth, releasing it, or at least calling its apparent primacy into question, will increase both freedom and insecurity while reducing constriction. If awakening to a significant small "t" truth from a slumber of unknowing or ignorance, the effect may be dynamic and galvanizing. The "truth" of really becoming aware of something is often its own reward, and subsequent changes in life circumstances or situation, either apparently negative or positive, are digestible under the impetus of becoming freshly aware of a new truth.

H H H H H H

Passage #2

Lust (Craving)

Wisdom

Lust (Craving) is blindness, a sense of drivenness in which all other considerations fall away. The nearsightedness of conscious attention and focus reduces personal existence to the level of a simple yet very strident urge or quest. Complexity, complications and consequence are utterly excluded as conscious considerations. Sated lust, unto itself, begets more lust. Sated craving, unto itself, begets more craving. The satisfaction which one can't live without is that which denies a fuller experience of life itself. To visit lust (craving) periodically is a part of the fullness of being human. To get caught there, as if hijacked by a revolving door, is one form of hell. The capacity to arouse, to become aroused—infused with desire—is not to be despised. As part of a larger orchestration of human feeling and bondedness, it is a sublime accent and drive, perhaps even the first conscious acceptance into one's being of a locus of control and intent that may be experienced as "not self"—as not solely ego-based. This experience may start to open one to the whole notion of being influencable by other ranges of energies, rather than living under an implicit assumption of ego-dominance. To be possessed of lust (craving)—to have one's existence rooted in pursuit of sating lust/ desire as an end in itself—is like robbing one's own bank. Depletion and perdition are the sole (soul) renderings of any mindless pursuit.

Divination

You are either possessed, or in danger of being possessed, by that narrowing of attention and focus which lust (craving) is. If you have recently experienced a sudden rousing of this profound force, it may be time to consider the source of the energy that is fueling it. The source may not even be sexual or craving energy, per se, but may be, rather, an emotional current which is seeking to become conscious but is being shunted into a sensory channel. Stay with the feeling of lust (craving) and let it carry you deeper, without acting on it. It may give way to a sense of old deprivation and abandonment, or perhaps some other feeling altogether. The route to self-discovery is to follow the lead, inwardly, of such strident urgings. With awareness, balance will be restored. If, instead, you act (out) in haste, you may repent at leisure.

H H H H H T

LUST (CRAVING)

Passage #3

Love

Wisdom

Love is that expansion of being which lets us experience the interconnectedness between us and another, and even all others, within a context of the universal striving of all incarnate beings towards completion and return-to-the-source. It is an energy that is operative at all levels of being. The force of love is awesome. It has the power to dispel all darkness—not by destroying it, but by transforming it. To love unconditionally—with an open hand—is one of the most noble aspirations of humankind. To the extent such a goal is ever realized, it as an achievement which runs counter to our fear/survival-based instinctual nature. No power has more potency in leading a person to radically redefine who she/he experiences her/himself to be. Even the so-called "lower" love forms—romantic love, erotic love, dyadic love—are powerful incubators of self-awakening. One of the most stringent challenges (among many such) that we face in furthering our understandings about love is in the happenstance when we apparently lose the love and affection of another. If our love is true, then we will develop the capacity to want the best for that person, even when "the best" means no longer having that person in our life in ways which we have probably come to rely on. This is a wrenching experience. However, if this kind of unconditional love can triumph, it is liberating, and ultimately healing as it leads us to an experience of love as a transpersonal energy. And that experience (often solitary), however it reaches us, reveals love to us as *the* abiding force—the one given—behind all creation, to which we are thoroughly connected through the marrow and to the core.

Divination

You are being roused by the universal energy of love, even if in scaled-down/stepped down form. This encounter with a larger cosmic realization may lead you to radically redefine who you experience yourself to be in the world. Surrendering to the power of this experience may be at once "awakening" and frightening—even disruptive. Yet in its largest scope, love energy is gentle, forgiving and healing. If love is informing your actions, then any outcome is all right. That's the freedom of it. Open yourself to the tide of love, and experience the joy and wonder of being on a journey that is larger than any one of us. It will demand the best that you are, even as it continues to refine your best into something better.

H H H H T H

Passage #4

Hope

Wisdom

At its best a way of X-raying the future and feeling the presence of a divine promise, at its worst an exercise in self-pep-talk delusion—an emotionalism masquerading as faith—hope is perhaps the least tangible, yet most timely, of experiences. To be without hope is to fall into the abyss, and even through it (which, paradoxically, may lead to hope). The hope which has expectations attached to it, such as being spared some form of catastrophe, can often lead to God-bargains. The hope that is less conditioned on being spared life, and more conditioned on finding guidance and a destiny in the process of encountering all of life's experiences, regardless of what these may be, is more powerful, and more uplifting. It is true that hope may arise in the midst of the most bleak situation, and shine as a beacon of sustaining light. The course ahead may not be clear, but the imperative of hope is to persevere. Hope can defy logic, the rational, the known, and allows us to sample on an intuitive level a reality which is coming to be, though not yet "here."

Divination

You have been going through a bleak time, perhaps having sensed a futility, even sinking into the slough of despond. If you are feeling an upwelling of hope, you may wonder if it is just a cruel hoax to be so teased. Yet you are not being teased. Other ways of knowing—sensing and intuition—are supporting you, giving you a respite from what has felt like a meaningless trudge. Within your fate there is a destiny waiting to be birthed and shaped. Authentic hope speaks of the unseen *yet still possible*. Thank God the Universe is more complex and intricate than you can know. There are many paths which can form out of this intricateness, leading you to the discovery of new meaning for your suffering, and deliver you over to your awaiting destiny.

H H H H T T

Passage #5

Evil

Wisdom

Evil is not the existence of a shadow, or "dark side." Evil, at its roots, stems from living in ignorance of the existence of one's shadow or dark side. Evil is the outworking of both this ignorance, and the "choice"—always operative on some level—to remain ignorant. Evil can manifest as malevolence by design. The clasping tendentiousness of seduction is always born of ignorance. The possibility of gaining some limited self-advantage obliterates a felt sense of one's place within the larger tapestry of being. Evil must conspire in order to continue to outflank its own fear. Its strategies always involve control in order to gain a shortsighted advantage, a "getting away with something" that "no one will ever know." Evil is the ends justifying the means, and the "ends" are often draped in language of spiritual pursuit, political "correctness" or societal necessity. Evil involves "setting people up" and "tearing people down"—destroying people—usually by intention, often by subterfuge. It infuses the dishonesties and hypocrisies operative at all levels of life. No one, in human form, is immune to being preyed upon by the evil contrivances of others. No one is spared the experience, at some point in life, of being a promulgator of evilness—of vileness—at some level, towards another. Ignorance of the evil potential latent in us all only compounds the problem and propagates its effects. The most common guises under which evil masquerades? Self-righteousness, and allegiance to a cause.

Divination

You are either caught up in some evil design in which an "end" appears to justify a means, or you are caught in an evil web spun by another or some others. In either case, you are called upon to awaken to the presence of evil as a real potential within you, and to balance or offset it through the process of becoming aware of it. Regarding countering evil that appears to arise externally, try to see it as a projection of your own dark potential. The evil that does manifest as if from without may have to run its course, during which you will have to learn to wait it out. Try not to vanquish this evil by impulsive actions or by acts of martyrdom. Withstanding external evil is very useful in teaching oneself how to bear with negative tides and currents without unnecessarily compounding them. One discovers a priceless inner stamina through proceeding in this way. Even evil must, sooner or later, relinquish its grip, and will do so provided you don't go out of your way to serve yourself up as its victim. Learning to coexist with evil requires utter discipline.

H H H T H H

EVIL

Passage #6

Gestation

Wisdom

Gestation is creation in the act of formation. It cannot be rushed, but is an interlude with its own special ambience and characteristics. It is something to be appreciated unto itself. The time of waiting embodies all the hope and apprehensions one must project into the unknown outcome. Yet gestation is not empty waiting. It is the inward turning-over and massing, even brooding, which intuits the ripening: that one is in the flow of a becoming, and that this becoming has, in a way, a life of its own—its own pulse, its own rhythm. Gestation conveys the feeling of some acknowledgement of a development which will come to term. The development leads to a delivery, or deliverance. Gestation is truly its own envelope, pushing aside the hustle and bustle of what precedes it and what is to follow it to establish its own groundedness in being. It is a beautiful time to participate in the formation of new life and creation, for which each of us is both channel and midwife. Given a compliant resonance to let gestation gestate, gestation takes care of itself, and only asks that we give it the space to do so.

Divination

You are relating to—brought into relationship with—the mysterious and often hidden generativity of creation, on any level. A life or a situation is in formation, gathering cohesion and biding its time until birth is nigh. You will feel and sense the weightiness and shifting of this development. Treat this as a cherished time—a time in which you shelter and nurture the unborn. The building up of life energy/creation must not be dissipated prematurely. It must go to term, and you must come to terms with its process, its development, without trying to force anything. Live joyfully with this precious time of preparation for new life and creation, as well as the ripening of outer world situations. There is nothing to force. The time is to be savored.

H H H T H T

Passage #7

Vigil

Wisdom

Vigil is a constant exuding of concern. Vigil is maintaining watch, bearing witness to the passage of time as defined by some circumstance, happening or condition. It is the presence of a consciousness which "sees" all, that knows what's going on, and it is the presenting of personal suffering as a form of commitment. Vigil speaks to a witnessing that is outwardly passive yet inwardly, spiritually, very active, focused and directed. It is an undergoing, fueled by empathy. It is a wordless statement of belief and support. Although thought of in terms of a passage of time, vigil does not know time, only purpose. In the fullness of its vision, Vigil, operating from a sense of purpose, triumphs over time. One cannot quite say that holding vigil carries with it a sure sense of accomplishing the purpose underlying it. Yet a purposeful vigil has meaning, regardless of whether its specific purpose is realized. Attention may be drawn to an issue, and if the issue involves an injustice, Vigil may exact a portion of shame in the wrongdoer, and in those who would acquiesce to the wrongdoing. "I take my stand, and through my very presence—my silent witness—I express my outrage or my loss, and no one is deceived by any appearance to the contrary as to what is really going on, and what is at stake." Such is the solemnity of Vigil.

Divination

You are going through a long passage not entirely of your own doing, and over which you have only limited influence. Yet at the level of your soul you know the larger picture, and your greater knowing needs to manifest as an attitude of Vigil, of bearing witness. Vigils don't always have cut-and-dried outcomes, but they are a statement of soul energy that needs to suffer, at least sympathetically, with purpose. As you experience Vigil, you will feel a solidification of yourself around something that matters. Although not able to force a resolution of an issue, your vigil conveys a sense of nobility of purpose, and the purity of your heart is a factor that will be a part of the collective energies which, in total, will shape an outcome. Hold to your sense of Vigil; it helps to define you.

H H H T T H

VIGIL

Passage #8

Peace

Wisdom

Peace is the inverse of orgasm. It is expansive and enduring rather than convulsive and ephemeral. That depth of peace that "passeth all understanding" is so sublime, so infused with a sense of the rightness of all that is, that it completely outflanks, effortlessly, all logic or drama to the contrary. To reside in peace is to know the timeless beauty behind all creation. Peace is not just the absence of dynamic activity; it is its own way of knowing and perceiving. It takes the sharp edges off everything, and leads us into our deepest sense of universal belonging. Peace arises, sui generis. It cannot be forced, manipulated, or bargained with. It is God's breath. The wisdom of the ages holds the experience of inner peace—the lack of conflict at all levels—as being the most cherished of all experienceable realities. It lacks for nothing. It is self-validating. Its efflorescence whispers of an entirely transcendent context in which all human experience takes place. Its sense of beauty and tranquility surpasses all considerations stemming from moral, legal, ethical, and psychological ways of sizing up and assessing. The deep repose which peace is arises from the unfathomable, pointing beyond itself to the unknowable ground of our being. We are deeply blessed by it.

Divination

You may come into an unheralded and utterly unanticipated experience of peace—that beacon of the rightness of all that you are and are encountering on your path, notwithstanding apparently unresolvable turmoil and irreconcilable conflicts which often beset you in purely human affairs. Breathe in this majestic intimation of the soul's ultimate repose, of its place of belonging in the context of the Universal. Savor the sure knowledge of rightness. Let "the peace that passeth all understanding" arise and fall as it will, and relish that deepening of connection with the Divine of which this experience is a harbinger. Peace will show you that this aspect of existence we term our particular lifetime is gently held within a larger, purposeful mosaic of being.

H H H T T

Passage #9

Renewal

Wisdom

Renewal reaches us through gentleness. It is what remains after a storm passes through, waiting to reconstitute, recollect, resume. Renewal is an oft-kept secret. It takes root in the deepest recesses of the psyche and may not even be discernible as an outer world unfoldment until it is inwardly well along in its development. Yet the power in renewal is profound. All those old battlegrounds now become bucolic parks and nature sanctuaries speak to this remarkable regenerative impetus. Fortunately, this deep stirring of promise and possibility for the future is not, at the outset, dependent upon any resolve of local will or willfulness. It arises mysteriously from its own source, and we, sometimes enthusiastically, sometimes distrustingly, recognize its current when evidence mounts that something new is insisting on seeking manifestation in our lives. This is especially disconcerting if we have felt beyond hope of any redemption. The epiphany of the eternally new—of renewal—is a part of our soul's mystery.

Divination

You are either experiencing outward signs of new awakenings in your life, or you are put on notice, notwithstanding any immediate evidence to the contrary (especially if you've been through a siege), that a process of renewal, new growth, resumption is already at work deep within you. Take comfort in this, for the process of renewed life is, thankfully, neither dependent solely on your willing it to be so, nor thwarted by your convictions that it is not possible. Renewal arises within doom and gloom, not because you have ceased dooming and glooming. The possibility of a renewed life comes to you as a gesture of Universal love, regardless of what may be your own conclusions about being undeserving, irretrievably damaged and "down for the count." Trust this prompting from your higher Self that you are more than you know, and that not all is concluded about you and your life's meaning.

H H T H H H

RENEWAL

Passage #10

Grace

Wisdom

If Justice is getting what you deserve, and Mercy is being spared getting what you deserve, then Grace may be held to be an unmerited gift—a "getting what you don't deserve." Actually, however, Grace—Divine intervention—whether of reprieve, remission, serendipity, rescue or love, is unmerited—not necessarily because it is either deserved or undeserved, but because the grounds on which it is warranted are hidden to the rational mind. In truth, Grace is neither merited nor unmerited; it is, rather, mysterious. Grace speaks of a cosmic assessment of our local condition—our local plight—that so far transcends human understanding as to be unfathomable. Grace is a philosophical indicator, hinting of a reality beyond what we know, or can know, and hinting, as well, at the relative status which declared human judgments hold vis-à-vis assessments couched within the context of the eternal or infinite. The test that Grace brings to us is not so much to understand its origin or its basis. Rather it is to become open to accepting this gift *as* a gift, regardless of its basis, and regardless of whether we feel deserving of it or not. Grace can take the form of the simplest occurrence, as in a butterfly's alighting on one's arm, or the dramatic, such as being suddenly drawn quickly back from some precipice, or the unlikely, as in rescue from some sure perdition, or the splendid, as in a gradual, inexorable flowering in one's life of prosperity and fulfillment. Regardless of its form, one experiences the sure conviction of having been touched by a Divine hand.

Divination

You are called upon to receive a "touch" of the Divine, regardless of whether you feel deserving or not. Acknowledging this divine contact will liberate you from your imprisonment in a rigid, societally-rooted negative assessment you hold about yourself. An introduction into the realm of divine justice, mercy and love will help you to relativize your human failings against the backdrop of the eternal. This healing of self via an enlargement of consciousness brought about through a Divine intercession (of any sort) *is* Grace. Even you are not exempt from being blessed with it.

H H T H H T

GRACE

Passage #11

Sublimity

Wisdom

Sublimity is a transmutation in the deployment of energy. Rather than discharge life-energy purely in the direction of instinct (the profane), the energy is held in, and out of the suffering which conscious "holding back" entails, this energy is given expression in more refined, evolved ways. The process of sublimity—of sublimation—far from being an unknowing displacement of libido into other channels, is indeed an exquisitely *conscious* process. In fact the process of sublimity is the refinement of consciousness itself. This is not to denigrate instinctual life at any level. Sublimity, rather, enlarges the scope of instinctual life to include that striving for higher expression and connection with the Divine. It is not that all instinctual life be sacrificed to divine intention. It is, rather, that instinctual life find itself along a continuum of striving and expression that includes both the profane and the sacred as active forces in relation to one another. Sublimity, at the outset, is not easy to endure, though it is easy to launch. The simple renunciation or forgoing of any habit or dependency is sufficient to lead oneself into that state of initial deprivation that is the fertile ground for sublimity, provided one is dedicated to remaining conscious and mindful of all that follows, and to render it suitable expression in some form.

Divination

You are summoned to open a pathway to a direct experience of the Divine in your nature. This pathway involves, first, a descent into deprivation based on some form of renunciation, and then a determination to stay conscious and bear witness to what unfolds within you. What unfolds must be given expression. The ultimate experience of sublimity awaits you. It includes the abiding knowledge that one has journeyed deep within oneself, returned with a portion of soul-suffering, and rendered it expressible in some form. One retrieves something hidden, refines it, and makes presentation of it as a gift of one's own humanity to the greater humanity which is us all. The soul-radiance that accompanies this process is profound.

H H T H T H

SUBLIMITY

Passage #12

Hatred

Wisdom

Hatred is underrated. It has its place. Sometimes, a fervently held hatred becomes the first boundary that a victimized person, fearful of having been terminally maimed or crippled, can establish to fend off an abuser. Sometimes, in the absence of any positive groundedness, the energy of hatred can be life sustaining—can provide a reason, and the impetus, to make it through, to stay alive, to survive. This is the hatred of focused determination, not the hatred of vengeance. Hatred is also a remarkable indicator of our lack of freedom. The need to hate, however authentically come by, is the need to declare separateness. Yet the extremeness of this need which hatred depicts is undercut by a fragility in which the hated object, person or situation is experienced as having the power to steal, maim, cripple, possess or destroy one's own identity and personhood. It is the feared loss of these core experiences of self that makes hatred so necessary as an antidote. Curiously, with the solidification of a more independent identity and increasing evidence in the outer world that one has "made it through" to some form of personhood, the need to hate diminishes. The discovery that one has not been terminally poisoned or maimed at the hands and machinations of others is a liberating awakening in which those others can be left to their fate, and the energy from liberated hatred can be brought home to oneself, to increase the breadth and scope of one's own personal being and living.

Divination

It is incumbent upon you to acknowledge the hatred within you, and to work with it. As unpalatable as this may appear to you, this is the challenge to come to an understanding of the function which hatred serves, and to develop yourself to the point where it is no longer so necessary. Hatred that is not faced within yourself will continue to show up in outer world situations that mirror back to you your need to do the work which hatred requires. To acknowledge, assimilate and finally let go of this remarkable emotion—so preserving, on one level, and so alienating and destructive, on another—is not something to be feared; it is something to be recognized and understood—with compassion for self.

H H T H T T

Passage #13

Loss (Sorrow)

Wisdom

Loss is a stripping away of that which is not, in the final analysis, indispensable. Every fiber of our being cries out against having to absorb out-and-out loss. Loved ones (including pets), ways of life, places, cherished friends, family members, material possessions, careers, whole-hearted beliefs, allegiances to causes—all those people, qualities and participations with which we architect and structure our experience of who we are as individuals, as ourselves—are subject to change, to being taken from us by "acts of God," by disaffections, by shifting circumstances and stations in life, sometimes even by our own hand and design. Loss is so difficult to fathom fully because of what it is: irrevocable change—or at least change that appears irrevocable, for to be experienced fully loss must present itself as irreversible. Throwing us back on our regrets and malfeasances, loss probes our choice points—those decisions always made at least half-blindly, without due regard for the train of consequences set in motion. The acknowledgement of a loss which, in retrospect, may not have had to transpire is one of the most painful of all pangs of consciousness to which to awaken. To stay with loss without shunting it by some form of quick-fix, or indulgence, or denial—to let loss have its full say and be in the forefront with us as long as need be— is to increase the odds of learning a life lesson which will not have to be undergone again. With loss, the only way around is through.

PASSAGE 13
HHTTHH

Divination

You are encountering an experience of pure loss. Don't compound the sharpness of this ache by actions or activities that will bring on self-disgust or self-loathing. Let the reaper reap, and observe the ebbing and flowing of loss in its forms of pain, remorse, sorrow, emptiness, numbness, anger, and any other related feelings that arise. Those feelings all reach deep into your immortal soul and enrich it, notwithstanding the agony that loss is for *us*. Know that in full season, loss will move on, and that which most truly belongs or resides with us will find us, or return to us.

H H T T H H

Passage #14

Deliverance

Wisdom

Deliverance is seeing one's way clear of danger. It is the daylight ahead dawning on the heels of the dark night of the soul. Sometimes deliverance comes as an inner knowing that the danger is passed, a knowing which resonates in the soul even before external events would apparently support such a conclusion. It is as if a chaos of sharp edges—razor ribbon in ten dimensions—with successive, unanticipated flips of the cat's cradle, becomes either benign, or ineffectual—powerless to harm further, and a way appears to scale the prison walls and throw off the shackles of old oppression. There is an exuberance to be felt in the birthing of new freedom, of the suddenly unfettered path, of the first glimpse of a rainbow and the knowing of its covenant following the bleakness of unrelenting tempest and privation. There is rediscovery, now that Divine wrath has been spent, of a felt connection to the loving side of Deity. There truly are no words to convey the relief and bliss of safe passage realized, given the perils that have had to be endured and transcended along the way. Life begins anew. There is, once again, a future, and the present is benign enough. Life can be taken up again. The darkness is past. Who would have thought it ever could be so?

Divination

Your ordeal, your travail, your adversity are abating. This may take the form of an abrupt shift of events in the outer world that transports you out of harm's reach, or you may have an inner know-ing—feel the soul's knowing—of this deliverance even though outer circumstances may not yet reflect your attainment of safe passage. Take heart! The mysteries of universal workings will raise you up, will birth you from your ashes once again, and a future, even a destiny which can incorporate, not obliterate, all your past suffering awaits you. May you fill your new lease on life with golden purpose!

H H T T H T

Passage #15

Fright/Terror

Wisdom

Fright/Terror is the forced disintegration of the "managing" portion of one's being, usually due to an unanticipated onslaught of some sort. The onslaught may arise in the outer world or from within oneself. In either case, there is a breaking through, an inundation which utterly outstrips one's capacity to cope, and leads ultimately to a dismemberment and reformulation of one's identity and role. No sane person would knowingly choose experiences of fright, terror and panic, and yet the absolute depth and acuity of such gut-wrenching are apparently necessary to us. When auspicious (although they *never* feel auspicious while they are occurring), Fright/Terror lead, not to self-destruction, but to self-de-structuring and restructuring. It seems that basic shifts and realignments at the level of character can only be precipitated by shocks to our core and, much as we might try to outsmart fate by "playing it safe" and not overtly court such compelling experiences, fate will not be duped. If the Universe's agenda includes the removal of all blockages in furtherance of the increasing cohesion and integration of all aspects of itself, then that part of Universal agenda which includes deconstructing and de-structuring will find us, regardless. To volunteer for madness is madness. To face it, and go through it when forced to undergo it, is courage itself, and the only way to stare it down, surmount and surpass it.

Divination

You are faced with a turn of events that is disassembling you in some way—which may involve being quaked to the core, perhaps requiring a surrendering of some cherished aspect of who you have thought yourself to be. The feeling of vulnerability, of being laid bare, of not being able to survive the onslaught, *is* the quintessential experience of Fright/Terror. Only by its fruits (which are usually a long time coming) can one find a way to re-establish a new context for comprehending what this experience must mean, and why it has been necessary to undergo. In the meantime, try to take careful care of yourself, surround yourself with loved ones if you can, and look for signs of the reassembling of yourself. No matter how hopeless or "finished" you may feel, Fright/Terror are never the end.

H H T T T H

Passage #16

Resolve

Wisdom

As the deep, inner alignment of knowing, purpose and will, resolve is the galvanizing under the heading of a priority—that intention to see something through—to "stay the course." This does not necessarily mean that that which one prioritizes and aligns with will be what actually materializes or comes to pass, but with alignment—with resolve—the likelihood for such an outcome is definitely enhanced. Resolve is intention based on the deep knowing of rightness, of rectitude. With it one can stare across a barren, parched landscape and sense the oasis beyond the far horizon, or the untapped aquifer far below. Resolve can recast privation and suffering as talismans that are purposeful and goal-directed. Resolve is that power of inner alignment between soul and psyche that is more powerful than any adverse external situation; *it is more powerful even than fate*. With resolve one finally integrates that which has been at war within oneself; now aligned, one's being is unswervingly directed outwards towards the outworking of a goal, a "resolution." Impediments merely delay; they do not thwart. Delays become opportunities for Resolve to continue to gather, to mound up. Resolve is an indelible sense of vision of the still possible, in the midst of little if any substantiation in the outer world. Yet the soul knows. Resolve brings cohesion to the soul. Resolve is not hurried; time is its instrument.

Divination

You are suffused with that experience of your being that is more powerful than any external fate. Resolve as a solidification of intention brings to you a quickening sense of purpose, balance and direction which renders past, present and even future suffering as worthwhile in pursuit of an objective. This goal, the resolution towards which resolve is directed, arises within the depth and breadth of your being. It resonates in your marrow as being worth the sacrifice necessary to achieve it. Such an arising from the soul's depths, enlivened by spirit energy, needs to be heeded. Resolve can utterly illumine your passage—nudging it from one of muddied unseeing to one of vision. It is a harbinger of passing through darkness into light.

H H T T T

Passage #17

Heart

Wisdom

The path of heart is the path of feeling-in-motion. Heart is sacrifice—a making holy of what is right. It is a devotional path in which the values of feeling are given precedence over purely rational or logical considerations. The wisdom of the heart is the wisdom of deep, wordless comprehension; as a bodily sensation it is usually centered in the chest. The rightness of feeling, of knowing "right," is an emotional experience, an emotional knowing. As such, it is not necessarily limited to factors within a given situation, life circumstance or even a specific lifetime. The heart "knows"; it draws from ancient wisdom, from all the lives (and lifetimes) a soul has manifested, from the bountiful collective of heart-experiences of all of humankind through millennia. One can take refuge in the heart's knowing. Heart-knowing can lead to resolve. When a heart breaks, the feeling of Heart breaks through into awareness. Such a breakthrough is often necessary for those who have become disconnected from heart and need a cataclysm to clear out the blockage so that balance and correspondence can be restored. The path of heart is the path of love, suffering, courage and compassion, known to be worthwhile because of the sense of soul-connectedness that accompanies such a path. The path of heart is the soul's work in seeking manifestation within a particular life and time. To honor heart is to expand the scope of being; honoring heart leads to a grounded life, a life of conviction, dedication and commitment.

Divination

You are embarked on the path of heart, an emotional experience of a rightness regarding something in your life that needs to be followed. This emotional sense of rightness may fly in the face of logical considerations or conventional standards, yet in acknowledging it you feel more whole and centered, and this feeling carries with it a pronounced physicality in the chest. Heart experiences often instill a quiet courage to commit and endure. The more you honor that knowing sense of rightness— of what needs to transpire—the more whole and complete you will feel. Your larger being celebrates your integration of heart.

H T H H H H

Passage #18

Transition

Wisdom

Transition is movement. It always involves something irrevocable. One moves from one side of a great divide to the other, and the shift may be, by increments, almost imperceptible. But then a change in the balance is felt, and retrospectively one realizes that a point of divide has been crossed. Transition is evolutionary, not revolutionary, and yet the evolution carries one down a very different slope into a new watershed—an utterly new basis for experience. Transition whispers to us of the impermanence of all material manifestation, and much of soul and spirit life as well. Transition is a passage by degrees, in which, over long temporal intervals, nothing is left unaltered or unaffected. One comes home to oneself during transition, for the relationship we have with ourselves, though it may change in character through the years, is nevertheless the most enduring one we can know directly in the course of our lifetime. That which is relinquished during transition returns our energy to us, that we may direct it inwards where we recrystallize the self-Self relationship (often experienced as an I-Thou relationship). The further refinement of this inner dyad prepares us to re-encounter the world-at-large in the course of firming up our compact with ourselves. This renewed inner relationship between us and our more encompassing Self may then seek suitable expression in a panoply of worldly possibilities. Once across the divide, life reassembles anew.

Divination

You are in passage. Something needs to be relinquished irrevocably. This something may be a concrete element of life-structure in the outer world, or a cherished view of yourself or another that is no longer matching the reality you are encountering. Your transition need not necessarily be a stormy passage, but a passage it is—usually across a continental divide, leading you from one watershed of experience to another. Transition, in a sense, is ceaselessly upon us, and quiescent interludes, also a part of life, do not silence the incessant winds and shifting sands which serve our life's plan. Once accepted, transition needn't be feared, only acknowledged and honored. It is a carrier of the Self.

H T H H H T

Passage #19

Transcendence

Wisdom

Transcendence in its most generic form is growing beyond a difficulty or adversity which, in myopic form, has been occupying all one's attention and consuming all of one's resources. This difficulty or adversity is somehow left behind, relativized—reduced to a mere "this" or "one of those" by a larger perspective or overview. One's difficulties and adversities are not solved, per se. They are recast in a larger context which depotentiates them. It is the attainment of this larger view—usually a view that draws upon our higher wisdom locked away in our own unconscious—which constitutes transcendence. Transcendence, as such, is not a release from, or escape from, our everyday reality. Transcendence is an outgrowth of everyday reality which incorporates it, and recasts it, within the context of a wider and deeper knowing. In this regard transcendence is a form of "coming through" something—pains and trials withstood, and outlasted, for instance. The steadying dynamic in transcendence is that transcendence is always conveying to us that deepest wisdom that we are more than we know, or even can know. This wisdom underscores that what appears to be a compelling worldly context for our lives is only that. The ultimate, evolving meaning of our lives and self resides in the Cosmic, the Universal, much of which is hidden to us. Yet we may intimate such a connection through experiences of transcending purely worldly concerns and cares. Transcendence therefore gives us a buoyancy which, almost beyond language and thought, floats us safely across and beyond the storm-tossed sea.

Divination

All evidence to the contrary, you are sustained on the invisible current of the transcendent. Feel this connection and let this intimation of ultimate security, buoyancy and belonging help you to relativize worldly trials and concerns as what they are. Yes, they are significant life-based experiences. However, they are infinitely overshadowed by divine connection and universal purpose—which work to their own ends—ends that may be utterly different from what purely human affairs and societal values would have you believe. Make the Transcendent a more frequently felt companion to yourself. It is more readily available, with practice, than you may as yet appreciate.

H T H H T H

TRANSCENDENCE

Passage #20

Anger

Wisdom

Anger is feeling fried from the inside out. It is a mind-altering experience—a form of possession which in its advanced manifestation, rage, has the power to hijack the body and use it for its own ends. Anger is unavoidable; its presence reminds us, no matter how evolved we may feel we are or have become via following a spiritual path, that we are instinctual creatures, often at the mercy of fear and hatred. It is galling to have to accept the reactive, angry side of our disposition as a given in our humanity. Anger is routinely equated with imperfection of character. It is seen as a blemish, as a blockage, as a hindrance. And yet, properly followed, it can become a pathway, even a highway, to the Self—to a higher wisdom (however we choose to designate it). Accepting the experience of anger, and recasting it as a personal adventure one has with oneself, is one way to harness it. This calls for making a conscious choice to follow the feeling of anger within oneself, without discharging it on a third party (regardless of provocation), to see where the emotion leads. This involves the apparent contradiction of giving free rein to the experience of anger *inwardly* without letting it reign over our relationship with another (the more typical course)—victimizing someone else (along with oneself!). Sustained yet withheld in this fashion, the anger energy drives deep down within us and reveals its lode: awareness—memories of antecedent events which enlighten the experiencer as to aspects of the current situation that are so anger-engendering. Or perhaps anger, followed to its deepest recesses, turns into something else entirely, as in sadness, frustration, fear, loss or remorse. This is the riding, or harnessing, of anger as an avenue to self-knowledge.

Divination

You are becoming acquainted with your anger in a new way. Instead of being hijacked by the feeling and reactively committing verbal assault (or worse) on another, it is time to harness the energy of anger, and its even more toxic cousin, rage (difficult but *still* possible), and, with intention, let these emotions draw you downwards and inwards, so that the stridency of their urgings for release—for discharge—now thwarted in the outer world by your own, unconditional conscious resolve, may draw you to an enlightenment as to their origins, as enciphered in the annals of your personal history, and a recognition of any other emotions that underlie them. A great adventure awaits you should you decide to undertake this. If you follow this heroic course through to its conclusion, resorting to it each time you feel the upwell of that destructive surge, you shall certainly save yourself a lot of heartbreak—a gain a lot of love.

H T H H T T

Passage #21

Rejection

Wisdom

Rejection is being wounded, or wounding. However, within the wound lies the discovery. Rejection always involves a portion of our identity that we have been depending upon the external world to define for us. To the extent that we are defined by external factors, just to that extent have we placed a power, which rightfully belongs within us, into the domain of someone or something else. Rejection at the hands of another, when it occurs, brings us up short, for we then discover the extent to which some portion of our identity is held at the mercy of another, and therefore potentially vulnerable to manipulation at the whim of another. This is not easy to fathom, for this process of identity formation is intimately bound up in our roles as children, parents, adults, friends, workers, lovers, and on and on. Our roles, and the identity that is derived from them, are so very automatic, unthinking and reflexive. There are two fruitful avenues of contemplation open when we suffer a rejection. The first is to experience rejection as a severance of a power that we have habitu- ally foisted upon another—the power to render us a portion of our identity. The task then is to reclaim this power—to "withdraw" it from the other and place it back within ourselves. This is painful, but ultimately liberating. The second avenue is to experience a rejection as a repudiation of some expectation which *we* have held about another—really our own attempt to form another's identity accord- ing to *our* specifications—and then to relinquish any further effort to do so. This is also very painful (punctured illusions and all) but ultimately no less liberating. Rejection is where expectation meets reality—where we meet the true "otherness" of another person, even as we discover the true "selfness" of what belongs within us.

Divination

You are encountering, or soon will, that cold, chilling stab of pointed, penetrating ice called rejection, one form of being slain. Either another holds power of definition over you which rightfully needs to come back to you, or you are habitually demanding that others conform to your wishes—that they should be as you would have them be. It is time for some reality adjustment for you. Draw back, lick your wound(s), and awaken to your need for greater self-definition—definition of yourself *by* yourself.

H T H T H H

Passage #22

Innocence

Wisdom

Innocence is guilelessness—being-without-design. Its beauty is that of being completely open to the immediacy of experience—to the present moment. The Universe becomes so wonderful and open-ended when experienced in such an unconditional way. To have this degree of innocence—this lack of ulterior design—is to know a universe that is full of surprises—in which the unexpected becomes predictable as an occurrence, if not specifically knowable in advance. True innocence is actually the opposite of ignorance. With ignorance one has a vested interest in "ignoring," in turning away from, a breadth of experience, a richness of savoring, discovering, and learning. Innocence is utterly of a different nature. Within innocence there is no pre-conditioned "shut down," nor conscious motive to avoid, control, manipulate, straitjacket, bend to the will. There is only sampling and wide-eyed openness and receptivity. Such a condition is more common in children than in adults. The alertness to being richly available to life in a relatively unconditional way, without conscious design, is serious play. The more one samples—discovers oneself able to sample—the boundlessness of life's tapestry, the more one's consciousness expands to encompass all of experience, in the eternal present, seeing within it the measure of one's own being, as gauged by one's very capacity to know and be aware. The arising of the unexpected is utterly commonplace in this dimension of knowing and experiencing.

Divination

You are poised to gain an experience of the Universe and your own soul—each as guileless, unpredictable yet magically bursting with the unexpected—provided you are without agenda as to specific outcomes regarding whatever comes your way.

Encountering the world as a magically improbable place, replete with love and humor, is a rare vantage point for a grown-up. If you feel suddenly taken to stop and smell a flower or pat some unknown kitty, returning their felt affection for you (one who is, to all apparent appearances, utterly unknown to them), you will start to slide into that innocent, unfettered, guileless side of your nature. The Universe is a treasure of enchantment when we meet it in this way. Every moment holds a recognition of eternity.

H T H T H T

Passage #23

Stewardship

Wisdom

Stewardship is being entrusted with the safe keeping, and proper administration, of something. The essence of stewardship resides in this question: "How do I fare in looking after that which is entrusted to my care, but which does not intrinsically belong to me?" Whether we encounter a fiduciary responsibility, as in serving as executor of an estate, or are given overseeing responsibility for someone else's enterprise, or even in the circumstance of looking after children, including the rearing of one's own children—seeing them as being on loan to us to raise, and ultimately having lives of their own to live, and their own destinies to live out—the essence of stewardship is always there: we have discretionary say over assets that are not ours. It is within such a context that one's own morality and ethics are often tested. To seek a limited advantage in an arena where one has authority and is not likely to be scrutinized or have one's judgment questioned is seduction itself. Life is so constructed as to serve us up an array of such challenges, and these challenges introduce us to our own split—or dual—nature. One side of us holds to high standards of ethics and morality, although such values may have been inculcated societally and not yet received authentic baptism within us via personal moral or ethical failure and its attendant suffering. The other side of us looks (feels!) no further than an immediate itch—usually a lust for power (or sensation of some stripe)—which can so easily be surreptitiously scratched by some little (or not so little) act of malfeasance or exploitation. Ironically, the miscarriage of stewardship, if fate ordains that it be brought to light, may be the most direct path to the birthing of a personal morality and ethics as real, internal acquisitions, rather than as an exercise in conforming to conventional mores and expectations.

Divination

You are being tested (as are we all) by the shouldering of responsibility and discretionary authority, and you probably present yourself, and authentically believe yourself to be, ethically and morally high-minded. And yet the "shadow" side, unbidden (to borrow from an old radio drama of that name), knows "what evil lurks in the hearts of men." Do you discharge your stewardly responsibilities with nary a moral or ethical ripple of inward dissent? Or do you seek a sphere of influence and siphon off some private perks? If you're like most of us, you try to hold to the former, but certain dimensions of personal growth may oblige you to succumb to seduction by the latter—and digest the consequences. Be ever mindful.

H T H T T H

Passage #24

Loneliness

Wisdom

Loneliness is the self cut off from external reflection. It is simplicity—felt sometimes as sharp, acute, searing, and at other times as chronic, dull, aching. The quality of one's experience of loneliness says volumes about one's relationship with oneself. Loneliness, as an active loss of something or a withdrawal from something, acquaints us with our essential condition. We are never far from it, regardless of external commotion and internal distractions. We can compound it by engaging in destructive actions or we can honor its simplicity through self-restraint. Loneliness is not something to be fought; it is something to be felt. It is not something to be curtailed; it is something to be followed. It may lead both to a sense of utter desolation in terms of personal impoverishment and to a sense of mother-lode riches waiting to be mined and assayed. To open to loneliness is to know the immensity of interior space. To stay with loneliness is to honor that space. Loneliness is not ever solved in the sense of being vanquished; it is befriended through being acknowledged and accepted as an admissible part of us. Its kindlier face is solitude. Loneliness speaks of our soul-yearning to find completion, even as it convincingly seems to affirm the impossibility of ever realizing that completion. The deepest secret about loneliness is this: if you attend to loneliness with thoroughness and with devotion, you will, in the fullness of time, meet the companion.

Divination

Stripped of that to which, especially in the outer world, you have become accustomed and attached—that which has defined you—you are left to meet the immensity of that inner void in the absence of what used to occupy it, or shield it from view. The true drama within life is to reconnoiter oneself in the absence of habitual filler. You have either entered upon such a passage or soon will. The old, familiar world starts to carry an estrangement with it. Whatever new discoveries are there to be made about yourself can emerge only within the chrysalis of loneliness. While it is so understandable to want a quick resolution to loneliness, and so very easy to be premature in expecting it to conclude, at its root loneliness is not something to be resolved. Loneliness, rather, is something to be digested. If you can encounter, and bear with, yourself at this level, relinquishing all efforts to force outcomes or clutch at the tethers of personal identity, you will know yourself with a thoroughness that is a rarity in these times. And when, of itself, the companion comes, you will be ready.

H T H T T

Passage #25

Honesty

Wisdom

Honesty is overrated, and yet it takes considerable experience and experimenting with honesty to come to know this. Honesty means, loosely, being open, without secrets. How possible is this? Experiment. One amazing experiment, should you dare, is to attempt to maintain no conscious secrets from anyone, most especially those who are nearest and dearest to you (though including all others, as well). If one exerts him/herself to be open—honest—in this way, noteworthy events may follow. One externalizes the private, inner life of one's thoughts, feelings, motivations and deeds by making knowledge of them available, without any holding back, to all concerned parties. This "openness" is usually a bruising exercise in leveling with people that, at times, can be experienced as "leveling people." Bear in mind that, while not necessarily recommended, this is *the* great experiment with honesty. Life does rearrange under an onslaught of honesty such as this, and it actually is possible to maintain a remarkable degree of openness—lack of secrecy—for an extended time, *and* this experience can be very heady, indeed. Hiddenness, secrecy, privacy, ulterior motives and designs, compartmentalized living, all appear to be undercut—cut off at their roots . . . But they're not. Two things inexorably happen. The first is that the expenditure of energy required to maintain this level of openness becomes prohibitive, and our resources to do so dwindle. The second occurrence is more pertinent, and relates to the first: our beings, at the level of soul and psyche, continue to generate the psychological equivalent of germ cultures which proliferate in the dark, damp recesses of our interior lives, and ultimately elude our conscious scourings. Our psyches simply refuse to be cornered or boxed in by our own willful attempts to be "honest to a fault." Wholesale honesty fails because in the end it is too one-sided and does violence to our own nature.

Divination

You are required to learn something about honesty, without selling out to it. Though a daring, sometimes necessary experiment to attempt, one-size-fits-all openness is a cheap out, robbing us of our need to develop discernment and judgment in our patterns of relating with others. Yet you may need to "try (absolute) honesty on," for a while, to see how it works out. If you experiment with honesty to the degree necessary to see your way through to the impossibility it presents, you will, indeed, have hewn to a remarkable standard of honesty to reach this point of comprehension.

H T T H H H

Passage #26

Rest

Wisdom

Rest is not doing. It is regrouping—but even this says it too actively. Rest is giving in to creaturehood, to the needs of the human creature to restore, renew (especially the body), release. Even waiting is an active posture of mind. Rest is not. Perhaps the paucity of language in describing rest says something about how unvalued the whole notion of "not doing" is within our stress-ridden, goal-oriented, competitive, sleep-deprived culture. Nor does meditation, which often involves active qualities of mind, come close to it, either. Even living in "pure being," rather than doing, does not sidle up to rest, because in pure being there is, as yet, active attention. So what is rest? It is repose; it is quietude on all levels; it is aimlessness-become-art. It is sitting on a lawn under a tree and not marking the passage of time, nor trying to solve *anything*. Rest is spatial, not temporal. Rest is giving over to the body that the body may use its own wisdom to restore itself—the better to be a vehicle for subsequent attention and activity. Rest gathers, quietly. Consciousness is not refined, as in meditation; it is suspended. Rest is not hurried. It luxuriates in the prospect of having hours before us, in which absolutely *nothing* has to happen or be accomplished. It is a breeze gently rustling curtains by an open window. Rest is lying awake at night, unable to fall off to sleep, and not even caring about *that*—for, asleep or awake, the whole night lies before us, so inviting in the fullness of its utter lack of demand upon us.

Divination

It is time for you to suspend attempts at self-improvement and problem solving, and succumb to your need for rest and restoration. This space of rest is of a different order from everyday wakeful consciousness. Awareness can die for a while. You needn't do, dwell, or meditate on anything. No fixing or improvement is required. There need be no concern about cares or outcomes. A space of obligatory *nothing* opens out before you. This space fills you and, with you within it, is sufficient unto itself.

H T T H H T

Passage #27

Freedom

Wisdom

Freedom is the opportunity to choose one's limitations, rather than having them summarily imposed from without. Freedom can only know itself in relation to its antipode—bondage, and bondage's siblings: obligations and responsibilities. Freedom can be a terrifying thing. It is so much easier, in a way, to have one's role and identity defined by the exigencies of everyday life. Not much thought required here. Yet to truly experience the possibility that freedom of choice holds for us—the power to rip oneself away from life's stale moorings—is both awesome and awful. Safer to reside in the habitual rather than venture to toy with free choice! Freedom can never be granted. It can only be claimed. Those who rail on about external oppressors often find, paradoxically, a safer refuge in being oppressed, for it spares them the risk of making that personal declaration of freedom which is the only true direct alternative to living in bondage. Freedom can happen only by an act of self-coronation. While theoretically grand and ennobling, freedom always represents a stage of passage from one discarded nexus of duty, responsibility and obligation to another constellation of duty, responsibility and obligation—hopefully one more closely mirroring the priorities of the heart. The choice of one's next form of bondage is so imposing because within the envelope of the experience of freedom one senses all the unlived lives and latent possibilities pulsing, brimming, just beneath the surface, competing for manifestation. To stand suspended within this envelope of freedom for a while is to know both the panoply of possibilities which we could, in theory, follow, combined with recognition of the impossibility of living out more than the merest fleck of them within our given lifetime. And then we choose, decide—decidere—cutting away options, yet defining a path, and this thing called "our life" resumes.

Divination

You are forced to choose, though not what to choose. This is about as close to freedom as any of us ever gets. Yet within the pre-choice spell-bubble of latent possibilities and countless life paths, reside for a while, that you may experience your being in its myriad aspects of latent manifestation. The freedom to choose is precious. Options that cannot be lived out get slaughtered along the way, but that is the price (read: the consciousness) of freedom. 'Tis better to honor the existence of all within you that would seek manifestation. Even if you can birth but a smidgeon of it, you can continue to feel the presence of all of it.

H T T H T H

Passage #28

Despair

Wisdom

Trampled to the point where all tendrils of hope have been stomped and shredded, despair knows no exit. All paths out of despair appear circular, leading right back into it. All assumptions, all expectations, no matter how gentle or well intended, lay crushed. How can there be wisdom in any of this? The feeling of despair is physical as well as emotional. Although "going back to the drawing board" is needed, there is no energy even to do that. Despair feels like "forever." The question is not, amidst despair, "What solves it?" Rather, the question is, "What happens if despair is allowed to run its course?" What is it within us that has the power—and indeed, the intention—to counter, or at least offset, the stunning and profound experience of defeat which is written all over despair? Here is a true mystery. Why does our deeper nature, which indeed can move in mysterious ways to restore us amidst despair, seem to need, even require, that we in our more limited form of being and knowing have these experiences of utter hopelessness, of dreams, or past actualities, utterly dashed? If the experience of despair is so convincing as the "final word" on what our lives are all about, why is it offset at all—not by distractions, but by an inner knowing, even more deeply rooted than despair itself, that lets us awaken to a new possibility, and feel that the game of life is not yet concluded?

Divination

You are faced with a bleakness that feels like the last stop on the road of life. Hard times indeed! Draw into yourself and ponder other times in your life when you have felt exactly this way—the sure sense of certainty—even of faith (however inverted)—that life, for you, was over. Even though you do not have direct say over that part of your being which demands that you encounter despair, and which also has the power to vitiate it, draw on your own personal history to take stock of the fact emerging with vibrancy from your past: every apparent ending—every "death in life"—has given rise to the promise of a new future. You may stake your life—and your lifetime—on this. You must withstand the present to reach that future which, oh so patiently, awaits your arrival.

H T T H T T

Passage #29

Attachment

Wisdom

Attachment always involves self-other. The "other" may be another person or thing, situation or circumstance, institution or idea, place or environment, avocation or vocation, role or responsibility. Attachment can also express itself as some form of addiction, whether substance-based or behavioral. Attachment to "other" can be seen as constituting our fundamental relationship to life itself, where "other" is the circumstance of being incarnate in a body with an ego to protect. Attachment is the basic impetus behind all of material manifestation. Without the hunger to attach, there would be no motive-force to come into existence at all. Notwithstanding the plethora of attachments possible, it is sometimes useful to consider all of them as being different primarily in degree rather than in kind. Many paths of spiritual evolvement call for a minimization of emphasis upon bodily experience, and yet attachment is everywhere to be encountered. Indeed, it is even securely harbored within the very impetus to strive toward the apparently "non-attached" goal of spiritual perfection itself. It is to some extent a curse of the human condition that the human mind can envision perfections of being that are simply not attainable in embodied form, given the givens of what it is to be occupying a body. To wit: being bodily incarnate and experiencing attachment are synonymous, and, regardless of noble intentions, the ongoing correlation is inescapable. Indeed, the path of attachment, of being in a body, is the path of imperfection—and no less a path to wisdom and self-knowledge for that! One may sincerely strive to transcend the human condition, but humanness balks at being disowned, and must be taken along with us, whatever our aspirations.

Divination

You are called upon to deepen your understanding of attachment—and what it means to be birthed into an existence the very nature of which presupposes it. This is not easy. You will encounter the limits of perfection that are possible for you, given the givens of attachment and the human condition. Such an awareness may leave one rueful—occasioning a case of the blues—for all strivings for perfection must necessarily fall far short of this goal. On the other hand, once this awareness becomes a felt part of your life, there is a balancing in which you may actually strive less, and progress more. The knowledge that, despite one's wholehearted attempts to be free of attachment, we must always live amidst our imperfections, is one of the more soulful, and grounding, recognitions to have. To know this truth is to have attained something.

H T T T H H

Passage #30

Nurturance

Wisdom

Nurturance is that which sustains, or nourishes, and it also involves the decision to let oneself be nourished and cared for. Nurturance times are important. To let oneself be tended, to recognize the need, and openly accept, the assistance and sustenance of others, is to find our place in the human family. For those of uneven development who evince a lopsided, self-styled independence, the need is to be open to the succor of others. For those who never tire, or cease, to be "on the take," the need is to discover that nurturance within which can then be used as sustenance by others. Nurturing times are gestational, or perhaps just post-birthing. Incipient creation must be strengthened by nourishment and rest. Nurturance is not only the act of nourishing or being nourished, it is the environment in which nourishing and being nourished can happen. The health of the whole range of dimensions of being—mind, body, spirit and heart—is enhanced by nourishment received, or extended, from any one or more of these domains. Nurturance can involve rest and reflection just as fully as it can manifest as activity and largesse. To know nurturance is to know the full joy of both receiving and giving. It is to feel the immanence of the next increment of expansion and growth present in all moments and at all levels of our being. It washes over one; it arises within one. It is the respite that heals, the splendid action that awakens and informs the world. It always refreshes and nourishes.

Divination

You are encountering the quality of nurturance. If you are a wholesale dispenser of "fix-it" wisdom, it is time that you desist and let yourself be sustained by others. If you are independent and self-sufficient, a connection of nurturance will help establish long-forgotten pathways between you and humankind at basic levels of resonance. If you are primarily a consumer of nurturance, look around you and see where you can start to be a dispenser of nourishment in any form, and get about it! To learn to receive and bestow nurturance with equal grace, as the situation may warrant, is to breathe in and out the goodness which the Universe has to offer. We are both recipients of that goodness and channels through which it can reach others.

H T T T H T

NUTRURANCE

Passage #31

Emptiness

Wisdom

Emptiness is formlessness. It is cavernous space within an out-line that, presumably, could be filled, although it is neither desirable nor undesirable that this void be filled. Within emptiness lies the potential for all things—for all manifestation—to arise. Emptiness is not despairing, needs no pretense, lacks for nothing. It harbors no ulterior motive or design; it waits without being aware of wait-ing; it suffuses potential everywhere. Emptiness, not nothingness, is the final product of all breakdown and deconstruction. It is stable, lying beyond all passion. Yet emptiness is anything but sterile; it is positively fecund. It is difficult to have a pure experience of empti-ness for by definition we are body-encased, and in every temporal moment we exist in a world of physical substance, sensation and manifestation. Yet the tendency of emptiness may certainly be felt and known. It is that naked repose which is beyond all suffering, all loneliness and all striving. It is who we are when we are stripped of all worldly treasure—of all that we thought we couldn't live without. It is our being, unadorned: our being minus our form, perfect in its vacuousness, beyond the reach of all harm. To know emptiness is to know tranquility. To know emptiness is to know, beyond all worldly pressures and concerns, the all-rightness of self in the eye of our creator. To know emptiness is to know that there are many destinies open to us—that the still, yet dynamic void of our empti-ness can, and will, issue us a birthing onto a path, either new or re-sumed. Emptiness holds the secret of our existence outside of time.

Divination

You are making an approach to emptiness, either through a stripping away of all that you thought you were, or perhaps by a sudden awakening into the void which you are. This experience, regardless of the undoing or awakening that surfaces within it, can be surprisingly serene and pleasant. It is almost contemplation in its purest form. Savor the volume of pregnant potential that underlies you—that in fact envelops you. In the simplicity of this experience you can come to know the larger you that exists eternally beyond all defeat and success, beyond all sorrow and joy, beyond any one instance of what we call a lifetime. When you re-enter life again as a more active participant and co-creator, you will carry with you a knowing born of your experience of emptiness which will fill all your endeavors with poignance, careful reflection and—yes—delight.

H T T T T H

EMPTINESS

Passage #32

Anticipation

Wisdom

Anticipation happens just on the heels of awakening. A new current has made itself felt, and on a purely intuitive level life has taken on a new dimension. It is an infiltration of newness—of a felt newness—into what has seemed a hopeless, stagnant stalemate of affairs. It is the first creak in an impenetrable logjam—the first pure wind of spirit piercing a long, dark night of the soul. How to account for the experience of being reached in the midst of being unreachable? . . . Of a whole softer, gentler current of infinite love and connectedness finding us across trackless voids of desolation and hopelessness—the thinnest tongue-tickle of "I know you're there; I know all about you; I am going to restore you—to make you once again whole?" This tender reed of spirit contacting us across such a great unfathomable chasm of hopelessness and despair quickens the soul. Life becomes a sea of felt possibilities again, even in the midst of apparently unaltered externals. Yet anticipation is real. An unnamable ingredient has been added to the mix. Life is to be taken up again. How can one place much stock in a purely inner experience of this sort? Could this not be merely delusion? It is not. Proof? It arises of itself, unbidden, unexpected: no pep talks, no fervent adoration of the magi, no quid pro quos. When it is "our turn" to be found by spirit, spirit finds us, no matter who we are, where we are, what we have done, or what has been done to us. Perhaps the greatest unvoiceable knowing encoded in being reached by spirit is that the Universe has forgiven us, and is about to raise us up again.

Divination

You have been reached by a tendril of spirit—a harbinger of a fullness that can start to gather within you. The dark night of the soul is passing. Pure joy and inner (contained) elation are elements in the anticipation of how this blessedness will gain an outworking in your life. This awareness of blessed connection with the more encompassing reality which is the Universe breaks a long, long dry spell for you. Others will notice this change about you but won't know how to describe it. A general lightening is happening. Sweet anticipation as to what all this could mean to your present life is lovely to reflect on, indeed.

H T T T T

Passage #33

Guile

Wisdom

Guile is deception by design. It embodies the sense of ulterior motive and focused duplicity. It is also sometimes necessary. It is a sorry truth that not everyone holds our own best interests, or those of the ones we love, closest to heart. Life in many respects is Darwinian and predatory. The waters, at times, abound with "Great Whites." Human justice also has its foibles, balancing as it does on the vagaries of human ethics, morality and jurisprudence. To be without guile—to have no ability to use guile in selective and necessary ways—is to serve oneself up as a meal for others to munch on. In a perfect world, perhaps, guilelessness would guilelessly prevail. In our imperfect world—the school in which we apparently find ourselves—we are obliged, notwithstanding conventional opining about the disagreeable aspects of guile, to make our peace with this side of our nature. At its best, guile has unique, protective qualities that can be brought to bear in no other way. At its worst guile becomes wholesale fraudulence in which all moral and ethical compass is lost. To learn to utilize guile like some lethal drug which, when applied sparingly and very selectively, has the power to break the persistent fever—to suddenly "right" things that have been upended due to predation by others—this is the true deployment of guile. Guile is a part of our nature whether we like it or not, and must be reconnoitered and integrated, rather than disowned as alien to our constitution.

Divination

You are due to encounter this peculiarity called guile—a quality no one brags about having—yet something which, in the fullness of self-knowledge, must be surveyed, and even employed. To knowingly deceive runs so counter to our prevailing, consensually endorsed societal values that it may feel intimidating to discover your own guilefulness and, subsequently, be faced with the need to use it. Yet a situation is forthcoming in which this will be the case. The intentional use of guile will create tensions of conscience that will help you more fully articulate your individual values as distinct from collective mores. Remember that the fullest, most realized "you" transcends, by way of inclusion, all collective/societal systems of ethics and morality.

T H H H H H

Passage #34

Celibacy (Abstinence)

Wisdom

Celibacy (Abstinence) is paring down. It is finding an anchor for personal identity that is not inclusive of some activity or indulgence. Celibacy (Abstinence) leads to a radical discovery—a new experience of the self. The fiber and sinew of character come to the foreground. Empathy has a chance to expand into broad-based compassion. There is more pure being and a reduction in deprivation-based craving. The spirit starts to sparkle. Something kindles. Life "lifts off," breaking the gravity of earth-bound exploitation and competition, and heads towards the firmament of service to others. The "personal" fractures; the transpersonal—the night sky of eternity normally invisible in the intensity and heat of the noonday sun—twinkles in ever present manifestation. Celibacy (Abstinence) is a journey, and journeys come in all shapes and sizes. Whether a short "break in the action," an extended retreat, or an evolvement over months and years, Celibacy (Abstinence) grants us an opportunity to knowingly forgo—to elect to forgo—that which in the end is to be relinquished regardless of our consent. Celibacy (Abstinence) is to lay a foundation, to set an anchorage in the non-material realm in which one discovers a home base in a place and a way of life where one never thought it would be discovered. To befriend Celibacy (Abstinence) is to open a channel through which one's life priorities can explicate themselves with sometimes startling clarity. It is to trust those priorities that shine through during such times—to know beyond question that one has contacted the bedrock of the Self.

Divination

You are in tune with the emergent adventure of self-discovery, as pushed along by an elective renunciation of active sexual engagement or some other form of indulgence. Your choice of celibacy (abstinence), for however long it needs to last, need not be a choice to embrace a philosophy of self-denial, per se. You may find that you are "backing into it," as you choose to forgo alluring situations that, in the marrow of your soul, you know would be only exploitive. You discover (perhaps to your own surprise) that you are losing your taste for exploitation. The sea of the unknown awaits, but your soul, enlivened by spirit, will guide you to the lessons and awarenesses you need to assimilate during this precious time. Your essence will start to reveal itself in more rarefied ways.

T H H H H T

CELIBACY (ABSITNENCE)

Passage #35

Bliss

Wisdom

Bliss is being on one's thread—on one's path of destiny—*and knowing it*. There is rightness everywhere. Everything is as it should be, notwithstanding any apparent situational glitches to the contrary. Bliss is seeing, or intuiting, what lies beyond the far horizon, knowing that one is integrally in relation with the scheme of things, having a sense of belonging to all of it: nothing out of place, nothing to strive for. One is absorbed into the emergent field of the Universe. There is no here or there, no up or down, no before or after. There is, rather, the immediacy of communion with the present moment, with the immensity of all that is—macrocosmic, microcosmic—and everywhere, all places and all times, in between. "Nowhere" becomes "now here." Bliss lacks for nothing. Its arising is not well correlated with either worldly victory or defeat, since it can recognize itself in either. Bliss is delight—which can delight in its own ability to experience delight. Bliss, second only to peace, is the most deeply felt harmony available to humankind. Yet bliss carries more of a surge with it—is more enthusiastic, more rousing—has more need to share its joy. With bliss one is still in the movement, and the path to becoming is as wide as the warm gulf waters which lovingly fill the space between two opposing peninsulas. Bliss is an inwardly sourced state that brims out and over, permeating the glow of our concentric auras of life—of mind, body, spirit and heart.

Divination

You are evoked into a blissful reframing of your life and circumstances—your reality. Regardless of external factors, the glow of bliss effervesces, charging your aura and communicating a sense of exuberance—even without its being verbalized—to those around you. You are the one most in need of recognizing the magnificence of bliss, of acknowledging its capacity to arise unbidden, regardless of any apparent successes or failures you are otherwise encountering. That sure knowledge of universal connectedness, of knowingly being in the flow of your own precious destiny—the rightness of your relating within the Cosmos—is its own reward, and lacks for nothing. Whether bliss is of some duration or merely evanescent, it is timeless while it is here—and it will return.

T H H H T H

BLISS

Passage #36

Vocation (Calling)

Wisdom

Vocation involves the work, or effort, that we are put on earth to take up. There are always trade-offs between the exigencies of self-support and survival, on the one hand, and the soul's calling to come forth into meaningful activity, on the other. Few people manage to combine, or balance, both considerations. However, it is important to try to do so. Vocation stemming from a "hot market" for some form of goods or services can lead to short-term monetary gains and material comforts—but with no sense of calling beyond this, the routines that go into such an endeavor become deadening and unfulfilling. Yet to respond only to the soul's calling for meaningful activity—for a vocation born of a sense of calling, a "life's work"—has its perils also. Few of us can be so absorbed into and devoted to a calling without letting languish other highly legitimate life-claims that are not, per se, related to vocation. Among these claims are the nurturing and cherishing of that which we hold dear across the spectrum of our lives, including being responsible to others who depend on us. Responding to a sense of calling can quicken the spirit, and it can also tune us out from other powerful feelings within us about areas of our lives which mean just as much. To be devoid of a sense of calling is to live in a Newtonian/Cartesian, mechanistic, godless universe. To be entirely given over to a sense of calling is to experience a form of possession that may not encompass enough of our totality to be finally worthwhile. Perhaps true vocation is that refined product which is distilled from traversing back and forth between the apparent meaninglessness of unfulfilling, survival- or responsibility-driven work, and the quickening sense of purposeful activity with which the energy of calling can fill us.

Divination

You are in that suspended state between the thankless and the meaningful, neither extreme of which holds a final answer for you. You are always a part of the equation. What do you value? Secure routine? Honoring commitments? Fathoming a felt sense of being drawn to try something new? Predictability? Unanticipated developments? Can you stay wholly yourself regardless of which end of the meaningless ⟷ meaningful continuum you are, for the moment, visiting?

THHHTT

Passage #37

Betrayal

Wisdom

Betrayal is the shattering of trust or illusion, as precipitated by the actions of another. It is probably the most difficult experience to encounter, and looses in its train the most exquisitely painful array of emotions within us: anger, jealousy, rage, hatred, dismay, vengefulness, loss. To encounter betrayal is to be emotionally disemboweled. The structure of presumed security lies shattered. A vertigo-of-soul descends upon us. We are slain. All preconceived notions of safety, of our own personal inviolability, of our very seaworthiness as going concerns, are ruptured. If we get beyond, for even a moment, our murderous impulses towards what or who seems to be the immediate cause of our woes, we are left railing at a God who could let such things, and people, befall us, and fell us. Our notions of "being one of the good guys," of being divinely protected, are now just welts of pain all over us. Does one automatically avenge oneself in such a situation if one has the power, or opportunity, to do so? This depends. Who needs to be more chastened by the betrayal experience and its aftermath, the betrayer or the betrayed? Does simple vengeance truncate what needs to be a more soulful learning experience for the betrayed? Does no consequence to the betrayer (as might be delivered by the betrayed) remove a confrontation needed by the betrayer? Or can we see in our betrayer our own tendencies at work, for which, if we have ourselves been betrayers of others, we might also be in need of forgiveness?

Divination

You have either been betrayed, or you yourself have betrayed, or (if you are like most of us) you know of both experiences. If you have been betrayed, look deeply into the soul of your tormentor to see if you can discover yourself there. If you are betraying, ask yourself if this is a mark you want to have inscribed on your Karmic escutcheon? In the end we have no choice but to reconcile with all aspects of ourselves, including those that we project onto our experience of reality as people who "do us dirt." Through reflection and discernment (while living with your wound) may God help you find stability on such a pitching vessel!

THHTHH

Passage #38

Kindness (Good Will)

Wisdom

Kindness is such an immediate quality to practice, and its rewards are instantaneous. When it wells up from within us in all its purity, there is no crosscurrent to kindness. It leads to flowering interactions with others. It is the outward manifestation of unconditional love, although it may also be practiced regardless of whatever emotions are underlying. Indeed, the act of practicing kindness is to resort to it regardless of the existence of emotional turbulence. Yet the expression of kindness, under such conditions, need neither be phony nor forced: it is a choice to look beyond either a mistake or a wrong-doing, even when mistakes and wrong-doings may be glaring and cannot be resolved on their own terms. It is a choice made from a deeper awareness of the common substrate of all human nature—imperfect yet striving, striving yet imperfect. To resist the vindictive impulse and to find a compassionate basis for kindness is, at its essence, an act of detachment from fear, leading us into a recognition that a whole way of life could, unto itself, be assembled, based solely on the principle of kindness. When kindness is experienced at this deeper level, we no longer are "practicing" it: we become it. Kindness as a medium of exchange, based on the heart, can transform our lives utterly. It is an experience of the innate goodness within us—uncondescending, not holding itself up to comparison with others. At this basic level kindness—good will—emerges as one of the loveliest givens of our nature. Under its spell, old animosities and rivalries melt away, and the world's wonderful potential lets itself be seen once again. This inner knowing of one's innate goodness is one of the most self-validating experiences available to us.

Divination

You are being called upon to discover the kindness that is within you, and as much a part of your nature as any fear-based instinctual urge. In the outer world you are to experiment with kindness—with fostering good will—to discover its special charm and goodness. This does not mean you have to serve yourself up as a free lunch in predatory environments, but you will find a treasure in acting on the basis of your own goodness, rediscovering that it really exists. This is to be relished, and will form a basis for bolder experiments with kindness.

T H H T H T

KINDNESS (GOOD WILL)

Passage #39

Death

Wisdom

Death is the opening up of new territory through the extinguishing of personal identity. The territory which thereby reveals itself is only accessible through this means. "Everybody wants to get to Heaven, but no one's willing to die first," goes the expression. This is not a call to literal suicide, but the principle enshrouded in the concept of death is, perhaps, the most universal one we possess, and Death is the most powerful metaphor. This metaphor includes much that haunts and terrifies us: decrepitude, cessation, putrefaction, consumption, extinction-without-a-trace, the unknown. Yet Universal Intelligence transcends even death. If we would but consider: in the Kalahari Desert of Southern Africa there resides a plant that grows and clusters in large colonies. In the dry season the plant withers and dies, contracting as it desiccates into a tightly cocked spring. The only germ of apparent life is in the seeds which are encased in the catapult arm of the spring. The plant otherwise is stone cold dead. When the first drops of rain, so very infrequent, hit the dead plant, the coiled up, compressed tension of the "dead" spring unleashes with explosive force, and the seeds are projected far enough beyond the colony to reach new territory and germinate. So it is that the intelligence of this species employs the "death form" of the plant in propagating the continuation of its life form; thus the intelligence of this species uses both what we call the life form and the death form to achieve its aims. This intelligence therefore transcends both the life and death forms. May we not derive from this prosaic example a consolation for us, in our frail state of physical embodiment, that a presiding intelligence shapes our destiny, employing both our "life form" and our "death form" to this end?

Divination

You are dying, perhaps literally, and figuratively, absolutely. There is no way station here. "Dying" forces God's hand to redefine you in ways that may not even be recognizable as "you." Your worldly riches are to be left behind; your "richness" will go with you. Are you open to this re-membering of your being, which includes both the "life" (incarnate) form and the "death" (discarnate) form? Are you open to discovering that the sum of you is greater than the life form and the death form combined? Are you open to entering that rarefied territory only accessible through the molting of personal identity? This is not a call for you to literally take your life; this is a call to be open to that remarkable life process called "death."

T H H T T H

Passage #40

Polarity

Wisdom

As the tension existing between opposing forces, polarity is that differential—that potential—which makes flow, or development, possible. Polarities are constructs of the human mind and, as such, reveal more to us about our thought-architecture and the structure of our psyches than about any objective reality external to ourselves. Holistic models of wholeness all point to the integration of darkness and light into that unity which is beyond both. Other models of wholeness and unity that seek to extol the virtues of light only, and attempt to banish, rather than integrate, the darkness, are lopsided notions which, should we try to live them out, do violence to our nature. So polarities, in the larger scheme of things, are complements one to another, in service of a larger consciousness, unity or possibility. This is extremely difficult for the human mind of daily life, which craves order, light, linearity, a sense of rightness and a strict cleavage delineating moral and ethical rights and wrongs, to comprehend. The counsel of polarity is to weigh all sides of a thing—to make a stand within the tension of polar opposites—to not act prematurely before what is to be revealed and realized can be. Polarity invites us to suspend our rigidity in cleaving only to what is good in us and disavowing what is bad—and vice-versa. It summons us to ponder what ills are committed, sometimes, in the name of goodness, and what goodnesses are bred, sometimes, in the aftermath of ills. There is a developmental sense here that some evils can only arise as a result of goodness, and that, indeed, some goodnesses can only arise through the course of darkness. The encompassing reality which sustains us all is "whole enough" to contain both light and dark, and this reality actively furthers the interplay between all polarities.

Divination

You are invited to reflect upon the apparently irreconcilable yet ever-present dichotomies of your nature. The tension generated between and amidst these polarities *is* you. Those deep, vibratory tensions are the circuits which infuse you with character—with tendencies. As you look to the outer world all apparently oppositional qualities or situations you encounter there are but reflections of your own inner polarities. Will you seek to integrate them, or let them integrate you? Or will you seek to banish, exorcise, or suppress the less desirable ones (in accordance with whatever you find undesirable—whether of dark or light), and impose a one-sided development on yourself, and upon the outer world? Polarity defines success not in terms of outcome, but rather in terms of the quality of struggle, and inclusion of that which seems irreconcilable, but fatefully related.

T H H T T

POLARITY

Passage #41

Generosity

Wisdom

Generosity is doing for somebody. It is as much a gift of time and attention as of material resources only. To this extent it can even enter into the realm of compassion. Generosity springs from the heart and may be opposed by powerful instinctual forces geared to self-preservation. Yet in the context of some aboriginal cultures, the Kalahari Kung!, for example, in which the notion of personal ownership does not exist, generosity is simply as natural as breathing. There are two wonderful ways to learn about generosity. The first, as an act of self discovery, is to seize upon an instant when someone else is clearly in need of some form of assistance that we could render, and, notwithstanding what may be an aversion to becoming a donor of some sort, to provide it, regardless of inconvenience. The second is to identify some clear need of our own, and then approach another person seeking her/his generosity in addressing our need. This action may even be more highly resisted than the first! So what can we learn from such undertakings? One area that becomes more elucidated through such experiments is the question of ownership. Ask yourself: "What do I have or possess which, in its origins, I was not given?" Of course life itself, which undergirds our capacity to "have" and "do" anything, falls under the category of "things given." What would life begin to look like if we were more constantly in touch with the "gift outright" that is the foundation of all that we are, rather than the more myopic sense of "mine versus yours?" How would we come to experience our relatedness with others if we were to start to forgo our narrow, erroneous, zero-sum-game assumptions regarding self-sufficiency and "how I got to where I am?"

Divination

You are being challenged to acknowledge what you have been given, regardless of what you place the stamp of personal ownership on—time, money, talents, possessions, career, family, and so on. Generosity then becomes an act—not of self-sacrifice, but of communal sharing of that which is held in common by all. To deny how your situation rests on what you have been given is to lock yourself up in the fallacy of self-sufficiency. We are all "Bozos (clowns!) on the bus" of life, and we have been given the bus, along with our bodies to occupy it, as well as the fare to travel. Is anything ever really ours, or are things merely on loan to us?

T H T H H H

GENEROSITY

Passage #42

Mystery

Wisdom

Mystery is in the not knowing, and the not knowing consists not only of what might be known but isn't yet, but also that which is unknowable, yet whose influence is nevertheless felt. Mystery always hints of a world that is more than we know, or can know. It is the "music behind the words" of our Universe—the nonrational substrate into which all logic and science dissolve, and in which they even have their foundation. Mystery is that which slithers around preliminary, basic assumptions upon which all rational, linear systems, either of philosophy, science, logic or mathematics, are based. Mystery whispers to us of hidden origins and meanings, and surprising connections. It gives the Universe its richness. Mystery always eludes being cornered. It is that region which lies ever beyond the farthest habitation. Sometimes it is that event, often unforecast, that upends everything preconceived and set in stone as "established." With mystery there is no "final word," no "winding-up," no "closing of accounts": the ledger is still wide open. Modern statistics places great emphasis on probability as depicted by the bell curve (the mean of means) with its standard deviations and confidence intervals. However, the true profundity of probability, as revealed by the bell curve, is that highly unusual, unlikely events are forecast to occur a discernible percentage of the time! Mystery, therefore, becomes predictable as something that *must* occur, even if the nature of any particular mysterious event is, in and of itself, unknowable and not fully predictable in advance. We are a floating lentil on a sea of mystery.

Divination

The mysterious—the unknown, the uncanny, the ineffable—comes forth to color your world—and shake your orderly preconceptions. The nonrational is the ground of being for all internally consistent "logical systems." If the Universe is truly random, then randomness itself occurs randomly. Hence, order and rationality must be naturally recurring features, among countless others, in a random Universe. Yet "order" floats on the nonrational, not the other way around. The imposition of order simply drives mystery underground, whence it finds new pathways to ooze into—intrude upon—our "polite" reality. You are suspended in mystery whether you like it or not, and you might as well enjoy it! Otherwise your life would be a bore.

T H T H H T

MYSTERY

Passage #43

Patience

Wisdom

The waiting that is beyond time: such is patience. It stems from an intuition of that which is not yet ripe, but is on the vine. The blinders we carry with us as an artifact of our corporeal space-time existence do not permit us to know all the twists and turns of fate which shape our destiny, yet the felt sense of there being something that is worth waiting for is always open to us. This waiting is actually a pro-active condition; though patience may hint of things beyond time, the passage of time serves patience. The fullness and richness of the possible never give themselves over cheaply. Nor is patience merely a contest of endurance; it carries an inner knowing of the worth of its constancy. The patience that holds the possibility of fruition is not a popular concept or value in our time: there is so much emphasis on the quick, the decisive, the dynamic. Yet patience bides its time, without becoming agitated. To know patience is to know an inner certitude; to know patience is to discover how to pace oneself in living through situations that are ripening, but not yet ready for harvest. Patience is a quiet virtue, so easily misunderstood as sloth or simple passivity; yet the wise know the perils of forcing things before their time. Events need to be unfoldments, not breaches, and in the fullness of time, the timeless wisdom of patience leads to outcomes of fruition that have enduring meaning and cannot be undone. One savors them all the more for the patience, as a resource within oneself, which has, with ease, led to the harvest.

Divination

It is time for you to discover the timelessness of patience, which carries within it the rightness of restraint, forbearance and tolerance, as it bides its time in furtherance of the greater ripening. Knowing patience will instill a new dimension in how you experience your world, including the stress-filled environments of work and (often) home, and (just as often) the process of commuting (and transitioning) from one to the other. In knowingly letting many things pass without pressing for outcomes, you inaugurate an inner resource of great uncelebrated power. To know patience is to know how to triumph over time—to know the difference between "killing" time, and "riding" time. To harvest the fruits of patience is to have let the Cosmos work for you. This is a sweet experience, indeed.

THTHTH

Passage #44

Vanity

Wisdom

Vanity is having an image to project—and protect. It typically places immediate concerns regarding appearance, standing and power ahead of more soul-rooted concerns such as meaning, emotion and direction. We are birthed into vanity. It is a trapping of our material lives, in which we strive to establish a permanent identity— a way of presenting ourselves—that can both draw attention to us, on the one hand, and out-compete rivals in pursuit of exceptionality (and its payoffs), on the other. With vanity we use external displays of this postured exceptionality to make an impression, create an impact, leave our mark. Vanity is "fart-food for the ego," billowing it out with gaseous grotesqueness, visible to all, yet containing only methane. Not much nutrition here. Yet a contraction of identity and appearance stemming from wholesale renunciation of those parts of us which, while short of being exceptional, nevertheless contribute distinctness to us, does not solve the problem of vanity either, because vanity can rest with equal comfort in the conspicuous, self-abnegating posturing of the ascetic as it can in the flamboyant gush of the epicurean. What "sobers" vanity is adversity, in which that which supports vanity is boiled away as superfluous stuff—baggage that no longer aids the soul in making it across the abyss. Soul can then shine, and vanity transmute into concern for that which truly matters.

Divination

You are being stripped of some of what you have used to project the image of "you" onto the outer world. This is, probably, not an easy release for you—however, if it is timely, you will feel the lighter for it. A simpler, more cohesive, more discerning, clearer you is waiting to be given form and expression, and a new circle of people who won't prey on you to one-up themselves at your expense will come forward to meet you—the new (or is it the soul-rooted "old") you. True exceptionality, as the part of you that is soul-connected, can come to the fore now. This is nourishing.

T H T H T T

VANITY

Passage #45

Reality

Wisdom

Reality is that which is, which we create anew in every moment. This connection between what may appear a "given," set-in-stone reality and the continuous act of spontaneous creation of this reality from moment to moment is available to us as we master the art of living fully in the present. To live fully in the present is to neither define outcomes (as in the future) nor to dwell on preceding causation (as in the past). In ways that are not well understood, but which are experimentally borne out—for instance, in the quantum dynamics of sub-atomic physics (on the micro level) as well as by research into the nonlocal effects of prayer (on the macro level)—the experience of a true present interfaces with time (itself a mental construct) in ways that can influence causality, "past" as well as "future." The present is the interface in which we can more consciously participate as co-creators in reality, even including what we typically perceive of as inalterable past events. This is a startling discovery. "Presence" is its own dimension, akin in scope to breadth and depth. With the experience of a true present—the gift of the present—we move to upholster an ever evolving reality, one charged with potential in every immediacy, one poised to unfold in quirky, marvelous, non-linear coughs and spasms, one replete with possibilities and second (third, forth, fifth . . . . . *nth*) chances. To know the present is to be birthed into the immanence of soul as enlivened by the spark of spirit. They are both "here" and "now"— both "present." There is no slowness here, only the joyful, exuberant bursting of creation, overflowing with abundance in every millisecond of existence. Only our recognition of Reality is retarded, an awareness that resides in a "future"—a future existing only as an artifact—a construct—of mind. Reality is already, and ever, here.

Divination

You are reversing your sense of causation, discovering that outcome can be experienced as preceding cause. As you kindle your encompassing of the present moment, your periphery expands to include an intimation of the direct experience of all-that-is, and within this, you become an architect of the present, which contains within it the future, to be sure, but, surprisingly, a fluid "past" as well. Reality, then, is a probability that can only become actual for you as you participate as both birther and mid-wife to its creation. A true experience of this will leave you struck dumb with wonder.

T H T T H H

REALITY

Passage #46

Consciousness

Wisdom

Whether birthed through pangs of realized apartness, or expanded through an experience of inclusionary immersion, *consciousness is pluralistic*. We co-occupy our bodies—share them with many different forms of consciousness, or awarenesses, each one of which is capable of working to its own ends within the body, with or without our consent. Consider this: the last time you were in your car driving from one place to another, and, rapt in thought, only became aware of the act of driving as you were approaching your destination, you had the experience (although you weren't dwelling on it) of being "vacant to the body," and in "your" absence, another consciousness, capable of negotiating the multivariant conditions which are driving, seamlessly slipped in and performed this function. Who was "at home" in the body while "you" weren't? Similar examples would draw on the relative autonomy of the consciousness of emotion and of the body itself, not to mention the manifestations of energies endemic to any creative process. We, each of us, are a *range* of consciousnesses, and the human vehicle is a transducer which scales down or limits the expression of those boundless energies that comprise us. To know the multiplicities of consciousness which infuse us at every moment, to know that "I" (the consciousness to which we habitually refer whenever we reflexively use the word "I" or our given name) is but one "special case" package of organization—no less a particular form of trance or altered state than any other (for any state of consciousness that is operative always views itself as the genuine article, and considers all other states of consciousness, relative to itself, as "altered" or "trance" states)—is the beginning of our awakening to the larger field of consciousness and awareness which can begin to apprehend the scope and complexity of the Self.

Divination

You are called upon to recognize the puniness of that part of yourself which you refer to as "I" (ego consciousness) and to acquaint yourself with more of the chords and strains of "othernesses" that, sequentially and simultaneously, fill you and shape your perception, behavior and awarenesses in ways you can hardly fathom. The immensity of you—your totality—needs a more encompassing recognition and expression in your life—which includes your body. Open yourself to that which seems alien, disowned or not yet born (manifested) within you. Ego consciousness, small as it is, actually becomes larger and more resilient as it establishes relations—becomes conscious/aware of those octaves of consciousness to which it is, bidden or unbidden, intimately connected. The more you can open yourself to those consciousnesses that coexist within, the wider the repertoire will be with which you play in reality.

THTTHT

Passage #47

Life

Wisdom

Life is always a celebration of process, of becoming, and every aspect of it is constantly morphing. Life arises in mystery and proceeds towards an unknown destiny. It is a form of consciousness itself, and its corporeal forms are carriers of consciousness— of ways of sampling and experiencing the encompassing reality running through, and transcending, all individual life-forms. The process of life exists for all. What we consider the good and the evil all partake equally in life's abundance. Life is the honing of transpersonal intelligence. It adorns, but is not limited by, time. It occupies space, and by extension continues to identify and take up occupancy in countless rarefied nooks and crannies in which it plays with form and adaptation. *Life shoulders us.* A hundred million dramas are played out within our body every single second we are alive. Life stems from the base, the root. It is grounded, grows upwards toward the light, downwards into deeper sustenance, and breadthens across ever greater reaches. All life—indeed, all of Creation—is related to itself. Unto itself, Life is exuberant. The impetus to life—that there be any at all—is in the mind of God. Life dreams, and breathes us, and, in Life's dreams and breath, we awaken, living out our little dramas almost completely unmindful of the wonder which carries us—which supports our being. The origins of biological life, and the conditions in which it arose—the actual stuff we're made of—link us to the sun, solar system, planets, asteroids, comets, galaxies and Universe. Through tracing only the thread and lineage of earthbound life, we nevertheless discover our kinship with all that is. A metaphor is a figure of speech. Life is a figure of soul—a metaphor of soul—a soul-generated metaphor.

Divination

You are needing to discover your kinship—that common ancestry, whether elemental, biological, emotional or spiritual, which has given rise to the form that carries you (and all other forms as well) and that places you (and all others) inextricably in the cradle of the Universe. From this perspective, sensed separateness may recede, and you may proclaim yourself a "Citizen of the Cosmos." Life supports you, your efforts and your plans. It demarcates your appointed rounds and allotted time, and in them it releases you to develop new forms that may sustain and give voice to your growing complexity, and refine the very energy of itself—of Life itself—that courses through you.

T H T T T H

LIFE

Passage #48

Restoration

Wisdom

Restoration is making whole, once again, that which has been lost. The rhythms of restoration are ineffable. When it is time for loss to stop, loss stops. When it is time for the certitude of quietude, quiescence arises. When it is time to rise from the ashes, a new being emerges. When it is time for prosperity of soul and spirit to revive, they rouse. When it is time for material existence to be restored or enhanced, developments reach us from the outer world. Restoration is part of a harmonic cycle of undoing, rearranging, and redoing. The redoing is *always* fuller than the former arrangement that was dissolved. Restoration is the rightness of divine inheritance, of receiving and being raised up by that which Heaven ordains and which is in harmony with our own nature. Certain things in our lives are fated. The cycles of paucity and plenty, of scarcity and availability, of destitution and restoration, are woven into the cosmic (and karmic) fabric and cannot be outrun. We are obliged to face many disagreeable passages in life, and yet the cycle of restoration restores not only that which belongs with us, but also our faith in the whole process of attrition, and "making whole." We can expand, with relief at our completed passage, into the restoration part of the cycle with an enthusiasm that can match, in its whole-heartedness, the terror and dismay we once experienced over our bleeding fortunes while enduring the attrition part of the cycle.

Divination

You are being restored. That which most truly belongs with you will be with you. This is a promise almost as a form of covenant. Watch how the phase of cycle changes from ebb to flow, from retreat to advance, from diminish to augment. Recession is due to be over. Recovery and prosperity lie ahead. Give thanks for the life that permits you to undergo such trials and emerge rearranged and more whole than before. The blessed part of the cycle may be trusted just as the attrition part was feared. In the fullness of growth and becoming, it is all blessed.

T H T T T

The Living Oracle ■ 137

Passage #49

Repentance

Wisdom

Repentance is whole-hearted suffering, in the form of regret and a willingness to redress damages done. It is a purge—usually a slow purge—of that part of us which has become soiled through a misdeed, or pattern of misdeeds. The process of repentance needs to be lived out and fully borne by the penitent, regardless of whether this suffering and purification are acknowledged by the damaged party or not. Repentance is, therefore, the new forging of a realignment within oneself whereby one elects to suffer, and to bear with, without recrimination, whatever consequences develop from the damage done. This process is not easy. It does not necessarily carry outer world rewards in the form of racking up points for our suffering. We are not always forgiven by those we have wounded. Yet the process is a healing one, in that the inner split, which pitted us against ourselves and put us at odds with our own values, is able to be mended. Repentance is long and difficult. It arises in the soul, which finds it a purposeful activity. Dignity, honor and worthiness are restored to one, and the coronating party which confers these honors is oneself. Repentance, living within the wisdom of "long sight," is an avenue to making just. Beyond it, we go on our way, chastened and wiser—and, yes, forgiven.

Divination

You are discovering that, despite your best intentions (or no intention at all), you have the proven capacity to wound, or do injury to, others, including (maybe especially) those whom you most love and cherish, and who depend on you the most. This smarts. You must go through the cycle of purging—of making just—which repentance is. With luck, the love of those you have wounded may come back to you. If it doesn't, you still need to live your way into self-forgiveness and the discovery of new worthiness. Repentance, in its full season, will bring you there.

T T H H H H

Passage #50

Perdition (Damnation)

Wisdom

Perdition is the feeling of slipping irretrievably over the edge, beyond which all is lost, and all paths back to safety blocked. It is one of the bleakest and most terrifying recognitions available to human consciousness. Perdition carries with it the feeling of being cursed by Fate—and cursed by oneself. It is a haunting: the flaw that sabotages all successes, which undermines all accomplishments, which wrests tragedy from noble aspirations, intentions and efforts. It is the upending of all we have striven to set in place, hoping, even as we did so, that those foundations would stand fast and resist our own destructive temperament. Perdition is the experience of loss of soul, of being beyond the reach of Grace—of feeling deserving of having to suffer without cease, of reaping—and propagating—a legacy of heart-break and shattered dreams, all occurring against a now bygone era of earnest hope, sometimes notable achievements, and (at least for a while) the conviction that we lived under the spell of divine protection. Perdition of soul leaves one a life-weary traveler, without home or abode—a soul-nomad. One collapses into oneself and finds nothing there to give definition to a future hope or possibility. All is a vale of tears and heart-rending regrets, without end. To know perdition is to know the feeling of having been condemned by God, and the damnation is heightened because one is kept alive to know it. Soul bankruptcy is as devastating as it gets.

Divination

You are encountering the bleakest haunting of humankind: that experience of what seems the certainty of being damned, often arising as the result of actions that might have been foreseen and avoided—but weren't. This darkness is utterly compelling and private. The "Hell" can be verbalized, but the immensity of the experience of damnation is one's own, and cannot be shared. God may have given up on you, but you can't afford to give up on yourself. It is of utmost importance during such a time to engage in small, yet definite, acts of self-care, such as taking a walk, eating nutritious meals and giving yourself lots of rest. You must persist. Through the experience of coping with damnation, you forge the deepest marrow of character and determination, and may even find the courage to confront God Him/Herself as your tormentor, as an architect of your torment—one who has spun you such a hostile fate. Have it out with God if you can about why you are so afflicted—more than once, if necessary. Don't worry, God can take it. (You're already damned anyway, so what do you have to lose?) You carry in your damnation a side of your Creator which She/He needs to have served up to Her/Him with forceful complaint. Confronting God is less hard than living with the feeling of being condemned and remaining mute.

T T H H H T

Passage #51

Compassion

Wisdom

Compassion is the gift of feeling another person's suffering as if it is one's own. The well of compassion is only as deep as our own personal experiences in living will allow. Compassion, perhaps second only to love (and they are intimately related), establishes for us the connecting link with all of humanity. It is a transpersonal, even a suprapersonal way of relating. To know compassion is to know of suffering as one common denominator of all human nature and striving. As humankind, the basic dramatic themes—story lines—we carry within us and live out through our existences are finite in number. Although these themes may receive highly varied and stylized renditions as they play out in our individual lives, human nature evolves from a common substrate that makes the experience of compassion potentially accessible at any level of being along our life-course. Compassion makes it possible to look into the heart of one's vilest enemy and find the root of suffering there, and to resonate with it, even if our enemy still hates us. Compassion which becomes inner-directed has the power to heal the wounds of unworthiness and self-hatred. Compassion raises love energy, that it may flow, and be felt, across all apparent divides of race, culture, ethnicity, gender and prejudice—the usual array of supposedly insurmountable barriers that are posited as blockages between us all. Compassion can be humorous as well as tearful, startling as well as with-a-sigh. Between intimate partners, compassion turns lovemaking into a sacrament. The healing through compassion is the experience of vulnerability shared—the end of believing that one is uniquely afflicted.

Divination

Your experience of compassion starts to rearrange your perception of the interrelatedness of all of humankind. Within a perfect well of empathy whirls a tornado of compassion, and within that perfect vortex of compassion you and your enemies are one; you and your loved ones are one; you and your partner are one; you and all future (and past) others in your life are one. This experience of compassion can break you away from a limited form of self-interest-based striving into knowing participation with the communal heart beat of humanity—the human throng—the human family. Compassion, unless you clamp down on it, will always beget more of itself, and the feeling that reaches you (for compassion takes in as well as gives out) will help define a much larger you—and you are ready to be defined in a larger way.

T T H H T H

Passage #52

Legacy

Wisdom

Legacy is that which we leave in our wake, whether formally bequeathed or not. We amass, in the course of our lives, accomplishments and failures, strivings and shortcomings, aspirations and broken dreams. Our legacy, regardless of whether we sign off on it or not, is the entire corpus of our lives, and this is left behind both in the form of gifts outright, and tendencies which are taken on (oft-unawares) by those following us into corporeal existence. Our legacy, as the sum total of all that we are and have become, is also encoded into the psychical fabric of humankind—the collective human soul. We influence, through both our evil and goodness—and especially through the quality of our struggle as we strive to reconcile both of these polarities—the ground of human nature, the implicate order from which emerge the individual souls of those who are to follow. This influence, or legacy, operates across the spectrum of human consciousness, and is not limited as an inheritance only to those who are blood ties, heart ties, or otherwise known to us. Since we are obliged to leave a legacy, and do so even if we think we don't, it is always salient to ask oneself, "What kind of a legacy am I amassing?"—and especially, "What kind of legacy will I be bequeathing?" Does the energy that seeks expression in corporeal/temporal existence—which infuses us at the inception of our individual life (the hand we are dealt, so to speak) become refined in any way, over the course of our lifetime, through the filter of *us*? How do we play out our life-hand? What lessons learned (energy refined?) are to be our gift, our contribution to the psychical underpinnings of humankind?

Divination

You sense the collective scope and impact of your life. Every thought, deed and intention, every striving and omission, every triumph and defeat—all is you, and all is what you leave. All is what is energetically fed back into the archetypal soup undergirding human consciousness. You shape the "givens" into which will issue the generations yet unborn. Known or unknown, you are the reality the other person faces—and is influenced by. To perceive the scope of your influence is to awaken to a new sense of responsibility—a sacred calling to shape your legacy in a manner that completes you, and contributes to the evolving destiny of humankind. Your life, your soul and substance, mean this much, and no one else's work can take the place of yours. The human family awaits your contribution.

T T H H T T

Passage #53

Creativity

Wisdom

Creativity is that energy—inspiration, insight, conception—which is subsequently birthed into some form of expression, and which usually, at some level, can be shared with others. Creative output always involves something new or original, as in an original composition of some sort, or a novel way of interrelating pre-existent elements. *All creativity is channeled.* The inclination in our own ego-ridden era is to assign our name to that which comes through us, as if "we" were responsible for it. Yet no single person is ever the source of that which is created. Channel? Yes. Midwife? Yes. Co-participant? Yes. Co-creator? Maybe. Source? No. We are arrangements of energy, and shape the energy that flows through us, giving it the stamp of our individual nature as it does so. However the energy of creation itself, seeking manifestation, chooses each one of us through which to incarnate a fleck of what is behind it all. To know the range of creative channeling which is a part of our functioning in life is to know the joy of divine connection pouring through us at the wavelengths we can receive, channel and transmit. It is also to acknowledge how limited the range of energies each one of us can conduct really is, when intuited against the intimation of how profoundly creative and extensive the Universe is, both in what is manifested and what is latent. To be convinced of one's personal authorship of *anything* is about as ludicrous as trying to take personal credit for the act of breathing.

Divination

You are being challenged by the two sides of creativity. The first is to exemplify the channeling or midwiving function in bringing to birth that special range of energies—in whatever creative form—it is your gift to conduct. The second challenge is to live in the knowledge that these energies are not sourced with you, but choose you as their conduit. This is so regardless of whatever the creative products are that issue from you. If you "learn your place" in this process you may be a vehicle for deep-reaching creations, while at the same time eschewing any inclination to boast or brag about what "you" have accomplished. In disavowing assigning yourself credit as "the creator," you keep your channel clear and open for further use. Knowing one's place as a viable channel which Creation chooses to use is its own reward.

T T H T H H

CREATIVITY

Passage #54

Providence

Wisdom

Providence is "being provided for." It takes a great deal to sustain us, and most of the time we don't reflect on it. Air, food, sunshine, climate, water, shelter, clothing, nourishment and nurturance—this list could be greatly extended. Of course, these needs, and the providing of them, are basic to our survival. To gain a sense of how the Universe provides for us can take a long, long time, for we appear to face peril at every turn—and perhaps we do. Loss of job, or possible loss of loved ones, or suffering injuries or illnesses that incapacitate us, or countless other lurking hazards—all these are part of Universal fabric, and they are real risks. Yet it can also be very revealing to ponder some of the big plusses that have also "befallen" us. Trace back for a moment to the beginning of some major opportunity, or success, or major relationship, and we usually find, at least in hindsight, a highly improbable sequence of events of some sort in which "it could have just as easily gone the other way." The typical discovery is that the major developments in our individual life—especially the positive ones—start in an unlikelihood and, once launched, become readily taken for granted as givens to which we attach some proprietary notion of controlling, or otherwise give ourselves credit for having brought about. And yet it is from the very unlikelihood of those events from which originates our good fortune that we may catch a glimpse of the divine Providence operative at all levels, not just at the level of basic needs. The unlikelihoods that hold the story of how we have made it to where we are now is the signature of divine Providence.

Divination

You are, once again, facing the unknown, probably with that usual sense of dread and foreboding over what can't be known or guaranteed. Explore the strange, unlikely origins of those major developments in your life that have preceded the current uncertainty. The Universe has always yielded up that which sustains you. Now is not the time to develop a profound, inverted faith that nothing further of a positive nature can ever transpire for you. Loosen your grip on what you think *has* to happen, and let Universe, once again, breathe you with Providence.

T T H T H T

Passage #55

Judgment (Assessment)

Wisdom

Three arenas exist in which we are judged. The first is the societal/collective arena. This arena consists of the weight of collective opinion, including values espoused by family of origin, ethnicity and culture, school, church, jurisprudence, periodicals and journals, newspapers and other media, politics, the government, nation states, and so on. Societal judgment typically gravitates towards lowest common denominators. Judgments label "villains" and "culprits" and attempt to structure social mores and values. Victims are to be protected (sometimes) though at other times they are blamed. The societal agenda is primarily one of judging and punishing. There is little, if any, forgiveness to be found there, and no healing. Collective/societal judgment is everywhere immanent and, hence, locally loud and powerful. The second arena is the psychological. This arena speaks of underlying causation in which things are set in motion in the unconscious that upend faculties of moral and ethical judgment. The recognition of the implicit societal fallacy—"People should be held accountable for backgrounds they don't even know they have"—can lead to some relativizing of the stringency of collective judgment. Healing is still elusive within the psychological domain, but at least one learns that collective judgments aren't the only game in town. The third arena might be termed "through the eye of God." Within this arena our lives are encoded in mystery, sourcing from the unknown, serving ends that we can only guess at (and we *are* obliged to guess!). This domain also encompasses spirituality. Spirituality embraces a way of experiencing one's life that utterly transcends both the societal/collective and the psychological domains. And, yes, healing is possible here, arising, when it does, quietly—in the experienced communion between the individual person and the ground of being whence she or he springs.

Divination

You are called upon to visit each of the three arenas of judgment. Perhaps you are thought to have run afoul of some collective value, or social mores, and find yourself in a maelstrom of societal condemnation. You are expected to weather this turbulence and to individuate yourself through exposure to the psychological arena—and to start actively posing through-the-eye-of-God kinds of questions, such as, "Who *am* I that this is happening to me?" What side of my nature is in need of balancing, obliging me to go through this crisis? How can I find forgiveness in a world which places more emphasis on labeling and punishing? Is my relationship with my creator dependent upon the collective's view of things? If you are diligent you will come to know yourself as Job did: as being worthy regardless of collective judgment, psychological judgments and the assessments of local gods—breathing, and partaking in, a spiritual atmosphere that transcends all of it.

T T H T T H

Passage #56

Promise (Fulfillment)

Wisdom

Promise is that which is, as yet, unfulfilled within us, towards which the tendency of our being takes us. In each and every moment we hold a potential within us that seeds future fruition. Yet each present moment is a culmination, as well—the fulfillment of many past promises that are now fully elaborated. The seed holds the promise of the flower, even as it fulfills the promise of the prior flower; the flower holds the promise of the seed even as it fulfills the promise of the prior seed. Life consists of an unbroken series of fulfillments, each one of which branches off, or "promises off" into unknown territory, only to lead to the fulfillment of the promise latent within it. There is fulfillment—there are kept promises—at every moment along the way. So much for the notion that life leaves us stranded and unfulfilled! *Every* strand leads to a fulfillment! A promise kept is a self that has ripened in some particular. A promise kept exemplifies the pollinated flower within each of us which seeds our future destiny. To sense, simultaneously, the promise of a future and the fulfillment of past promises as the quintessential feature of the present is to catch a whiff of the bouquet of eternity—such an amalgam of time and timelessness!

Divination

You connect with your self as the fulfillment of past promises even as you enfold, within the same moment, the seeds of future fulfillments. Within this experience of promise is the covenant your eternal being has established with you, its space-time manifestation. To show promise is to have been recognized as possessing gifts. Feel the quietude of that loving presence—the future you—who has (somewhere) already (somehow) fulfilled all your currently held promises, and is reaching back for you through all of eternity to love you for it—and to help you on your way.

T T H T T T

Passage #57

Rebuff

Wisdom

Rebuff is the blatant, stout rejection of one's overtures and affections. Where affection is well established, rebuff can enter as an epiphany of seasonal change in a relationship—often, but not always, spelling its demise. In such a context, rebuff speaks of shifting currents, altered needs and expectations between two people. It puts one on notice that the old ways of doing things—of relating—are no longer viable. This usually precipitates a crisis of some sort. The prior understandings and taken-for-granted, well-grounded arrangements are to be unwound to the base of the matter. Rebuff becomes most painful when, initially, only one of two parties is in transition. To the entrenched one, rebuff then feels like the rug being pulled out from under, and the accusations follow that the "rug puller" is being cruel, heartless, disloyal and senseless. Yet there is no turning back, only moving forward, into either a rearrangement, a breach, or both. Rebuff in its other face is that which we periodically encounter, throughout our lives, as we strive to connect with others, whether in intimate ways or not. In fact, rebuff is a necessary norm. It shows us where we belong, and *don't* belong, and although the experience of rebuff is always bruising, rebuff has the power to awaken us and place us on our path. To contort ourselves unduly to fit into the pattern of needs of another, beyond the range of normal give and take, solely for the purpose of avoiding friction, is never viable in the long run. Much preferred is to be rejected for who we really are, rather than be "loved" for who we really aren't. Indeed, loneliness is a small price to pay to not be abused.

Divination

You are encountering rebuff, either at the hands of a loved one or in your quest to connect with someone. Use the experience: examine to what extent you have been living in illusion, even delusion, about the qualities of the beloved or other party. If you are rebuffed by someone new, observe how you, internally, created a drama built on an expectation regarding how things were *supposed* to work out with this person. It is humbling to learn how we, emotionally laden in ways we may not even know, routinely invent notions of what other people are supposed to be like, and how they are meant to relate to us—often in the absence of any tangible affirmation by them of our assumptions. Rebuff puts us in touch with this inventive, troublesome side of our nature. Therefore, encountering rebuff is, in the long run, extremely valuable.

T T T H H H

Passage #58

Indifference

Wisdom

The opposite of love is not hate, but indifference. To be beyond caring, out of reach of strong, tidal feelings, is to find a stability where once there was turbulence. However, one need always ask whether indifference feels like a true deliverance to the obverse side of passion and intensity, or whether indifference is a residue of emotional shutdown, in which there is constriction, rather than deliverance. Encountering indifference as a deadening of feeling can be inauspicious, for it may betoken a dwindling capacity to experience a whole range of emotion. All this is to be contrasted to that indifference which may arise as an epiphenomenon of meditation. In this form, indifference is sublime. One retains the sense of passionate connection, which is internalized, but there is freedom from the compulsion to exact an outcome—to attempt to extort from another person some reciprocation of the intensity. Hence, indifference, in this circumstance, reflects a neutrality—even a non-attachment—as to all future courses or outcomes, combined with the ability to be passionately committed to whatever specific outcome actually does materialize. Life is not, in the meantime, robbed of its flavor or spice. Moving into indifference can be an avenue into experiencing the wider, fuller life, rather than a retreat into truncated feeling and expression.

Divination

You are finding your way now—having been buffeted within a labyrinth of passionate feelings, including both love and hate—into an era of reduced exposure to that which has been so upsetting to you. Indifference leads to distancing, where boundaries that have been sorely wanting can finally be erected. Indifference has a way of nulling out incursions by that which could normally seize you, stir up your intensity, and morally compromise you. You are no longer scathed, and this discovery is startling. There is change in the wind and that change is *you*. The calm takes you by surprise.

T T T H H T

Passage #59

Vulnerability

Wisdom

Vulnerability can corrupt us. We are all susceptible to things or situations that are our undoing. Vulnerability is devastating weakness. It is casting a blind eye in the face of impending destruction. Vulnerability speaks of traits and conditions that are life-long. We either come to recognize our particular vulnerability and learn to coexist with it, or we perish, sometimes by inches or degrees, sometimes by falling off a cliff-face into vertigo of soul. Vulnerability takes the form of affliction, susceptibility and frailty. It unhinges us. It is our cross to bear, our curse. It can lay waste to the most beautiful of uplifting visions, and invade, by stealth, the most fortified refuge. One can only start to come to terms with vulnerability by the open recognition and admission of being vulnerable. This can lead to the discovery of vulnerability as a pervasive theme within the human experience, in its own way a broadening perspective for those who are self-absorbed—and all too self-assured. The irony about vulnerability is that when afflictions and susceptibilities are openly acknowledged and disclosed to others who are similarly afflicted, or have equivalent vulnerabilities, human connection based on compassion and shared/equivalent suffering becomes possible, and the human dimension of being fellow travelers on weary, wearing, yet hopefully redemptive paths has a chance to take root. This is the hidden light within vulnerability, and a form of healing. Paradoxically, vulnerability and affliction may be as effective a vehicle for encountering and developing higher forms of compassion as is love itself.

Divination

You are obliged to coexist with that which, if left unattended, can destroy you. But take heart! Once recognized, vulnerability can become an avenue to the discovery of fellowship—of human relating based on shared vulnerability. The fear of knowingly having to tolerate personal frailty is offset by the passport to citizenship within the human race which this confers. Personal drama starts to lose its stridency as you discover, through your own affliction, the common pulse of humanity. Sustain yourself in spite of your vulnerability and susceptibility you must, but you don't have to be alone in so doing. In the fullness of time, the wounded healer in all of us can emerge with the profound consciousness that arises through the protracted experience of personal vulnerability and failure—vulnerability and failure redeemed.

T T T H T H

Passage #60

Community

Wisdom

Community is belonging. The longing for belonging that underlies community often takes the form, in earlier life, of Utopian yearnings and expectations—which are just as often followed by disillusionment. However, community, as an ideal, dies hard. It includes the notion of putting down roots, and feeling oneself sustained by a group of allied individuals—not necessarily all like-minded. Indeed, in authentic communities, most members are aware of their participation, as individuals, in the overall cluster. Communities are elastic—can allow great freedom of individual expression within a protective mantle of social nurturance. Healthy communities are voluntary. All members discover, despite their diversity, that their own personal interests are, on balance, best served by holding to community. Communities are networks, sometimes existing as cyberspace-linked diasporas rather than aggregated in a specific locale. The balancing of individual needs and community needs is a creative process that honors and values both the individual and the community. To find one's community as an adult is to experience a homecoming. Sometimes the calling to relocate is dictated more by need for community than by any other single consideration. This draw is equivalent to what, in earlier times, was described as "the pull of the land." There is a rootedness, a rightness, a feeling of "this is my place, and these are my people." In true communities lies the experience of being known, of being on a first-name basis with everyone. Community is the cradle that holds us. It has resiliency, on which we can draw, and to which we, by our very presence, contribute, oft unawares.

Divination

You still need to find your community. You have people around you, of course, and even earnest companions and loved ones. However, a sense of community, while inclusive of all this, is elusive. Don't give up on finding your community—where you most truly belong. Even if your Utopian visions of yesteryear have become tarnished and supplanted by gimlet-eyed realism, there is still a part of that old Utopian image which needs fulfilling. Find your community, or start your community. Even the quest for community can be a tether around which kindred spirits can assemble. Growing with others in community is one of life's great enrichments.

T T T H T T

Passage #61

Dignity

Wisdom

As the bearer of unshakable poise, the outer carriage of an inner certainty and rectitude, dignity is that quiet presence—almost a witnessing—the expression of a self-knowledge birthed and reared through continuous testing and refining. Dignity sees through things, needing only a glance. Dignity is quiet; there is a sense of self-governance and mastery. It can fend off all assaults. Dignity can never be stripped from one; it can only be forfeited. To abide in dignity and virtue is to know a richness and fullness in living that is a rarity in these times. Dignity is buoyant. It knows without speaking—and if it speaks, it is with the voice of quiet assurance. It finds its way by following the currents of good company. Dignity is never fully expressible. Its sense of knowing draws from a place that is beyond, and precedes, all words. Privations build dignity; self-indulgence diminishes it. Dignity can't be feigned. It is a byproduct of so much else: knowingly traveling one's path (regardless of where it leads), seeing things through to conclusion, a certain amount of self-sacrifice, a full portion of failure and redemption, a fullness in living (including serious play), a comprehension of where one stands within this Universe of ours—all of this and more expresses, or squeezes out, a few precious drops of that amazing substance called Dignity.

Divination

As you continue to meet yourself and befriend the one you meet, dignity grows, and becomes something you demonstrate. You may find yourself knowing more and saying less. Older forms of seeking satisfaction may be supplanted by the lightness of the subtle energy that arises as you continue to refine yourself. Others may start to react, or respond, to changes they see in you without being able to pinpoint exactly what these changes are. You will know that something new has arisen within you as you find yourself responding to situations in spontaneous, innovative, non-abrasive ways. You may also notice a quality of mirth—of surprising humor—starting to surface from within. Dignity is becoming your own companion.

T T T T H H

Passage #62

Eloquence

Wisdom

Eloquence honors the *word*, and the thought behind the *word*. Eloquence is not to be mistaken for charisma. Charisma arises as an expression of a deficit within the charismatic, who seeks to entrance, to spell bind—to bind by spells—the allegiance of another (or others). Eloquence is altogether different. It can only spring from heart-felt conscience, which seeks to channel the pain of its knowing in exactingly verbal ways. One who has eloquence calls attention, not to him/herself, but rather to the message within the words. The words, the meanings held within language, and the power of language to convey (well enough) the ineffable, all this is honored within Eloquence. "Words are important," says Eloquence, and the use to which words are put and the meanings around which words form constitute our common heritage, our common trust, transmissible through the word. Eloquence gives evidence of a soul's effort to reach deeper meanings, to cast a net into a pitch-black hole and, with infinite care, to see what may be brought up, uninjured. Eloquence may use few words or many, may be spoken or written, is always felt. There is a passion, with eloquence, for connection and explication, for loving dissection in the interests of the greater understanding. If the soul were to have but one means of expression—one language—it would be Eloquence.

Divination

You are finding yourself being more expressive in heart-felt ways, in which simplicity of expression starts to take precedence over tonnage. Eloquence lifts you, in moments, to scale heights of meaning and purpose—to knowing a larger slice of life. It speaks through in a firm voice, and articulates truths that are presented as self-evident, and generous. Through learning to honor the word, you become a vehicle for higher expression, never lapsing into charisma (which is lazy, self serving), but holding, through the word, a truth that transcends personality.

T T T T H T

Passage #63

Completion (Fullness)

Wisdom

Completion is the heart's way of saying farewell. The fullness has occurred; the ripening has reached fruition. We have expanded within a given situation, or within life overall, to our fullest potential, given the constraints that impinge upon us and the possibilities that have been accorded us. Completion is not perfection; completion is the realization of an inherent potential, as shaped by fate, on the one hand, and our own efforts, on the other. Completion signals an ending, but not, through any lack of absolute perfection, a failure. In fact, the endings contained within completion are the next sequential step in our development. The "complete" contains, and has visited, all the polarities: good and evil, success and failure, love and hatred, love and indifference, hatred and forgiveness, hatred and compassion, power and impotence, euphoria and rage (quite a dynamic between these two), ego inflation and self-negation, hope and despair, indulgence and abstinence, maleness and femaleness, and so many others. The complete life is complete because it has found a way to visit these extremes, and, *ultimately entrapped by none*, has grown larger and more beautiful for the experience. A complete life is a marvel to behold in those rare others who realize it—and it *is* available to us through our honest and open acceptance of whatever life deals us. *We* are the experiences that befall us and uplift us, and while there is no exemption from any of life's stages, there is a satisfaction, which is deeper and more enduring than can be expressed, growing out of the sure knowledge that, in our completeness, we have truly lived.

Divination

In the fullness of time you approach completeness regarding a chapter of your life, or perhaps even of this life-sojourn itself. Your completion and fullness bless you, and many others. Now is the time to savor the immensity that is, and has been, your life. Your completion is tailor-made for you; it does not resemble anyone else's. The Universe has created you and carried you, and in your realization of fullness you complete a portion of the Universe. This completed portion can never be taken away, nor diminished, nor undone. It is inscribed for all of eternity. Look to the counsel of all your years and the richness of your experience to find an intimation of where your completion will lead you next. Bless you. Many blessings to you on your sacred journey.

T T T T T H

COMPLETION (FULLNESS)

Passage #64

The Unknowable

Wisdom

The Unknowable is that which cannot be known. It is the ground of being itself. It underlies and envelops everything, but resists all impulse to be known in its native purity. It can only be sensed through its myriad manifestations, of which your life is one. As you come to know yourself more, you will draw nearer to it. Rest assured, the Unknowable knows you absolutely. The Unknowable also is our way of representing what cannot be specifically channeled through any oracle. All oracles do a certain violence to the Universe, in parsing it into a finite number of discrete parts, or concepts, and in so doing offering little sub-channels through which the Universe may express diminutive flickerings of itself. There is some hubris in all such efforts, and perhaps more than a little presumption. But the Universe is kind, and does not seem to mind too much. Wherever your unknowns and unknowables are, walk with care and keep your ear to the ground. Prepare to be surprised, astonished even—and hit blind-side sometimes. It is the Unknowable's way of keeping you loose, and teachable. No premature fossilization for you! The Unknowable reminds us that Divine guidance can use any person, and any pathway, at any time, to reach us. In making room within your life and within your soul for the Unknowable, you honor Universal intention. We are drawn and held to its bosom, and nurtured at its breast. Against the backdrop of the Unknowable we are all as wide-eyed infants, encountering, in each and every ever-present moment, a new lifetime in all it's immensity, so bright and shining.

Divination

It has been said that the psychotic drowns in the same ocean in which the mystic swims with delight. You know what this means. The Unknowable for you no longer holds peril; it is the ladle of being which stirs up your soup. It gives you life in all its inscrutable complexity, tests you in countless, mostly unforeseen ways, obliges you to make decisions when you feel ill-prepared to do so, and breathes its life through you as you breathe yours. Acknowledging the Unknowable will create life anew for you at every moment. And in the end, you will make it home to Ithaca.

T T T T T T

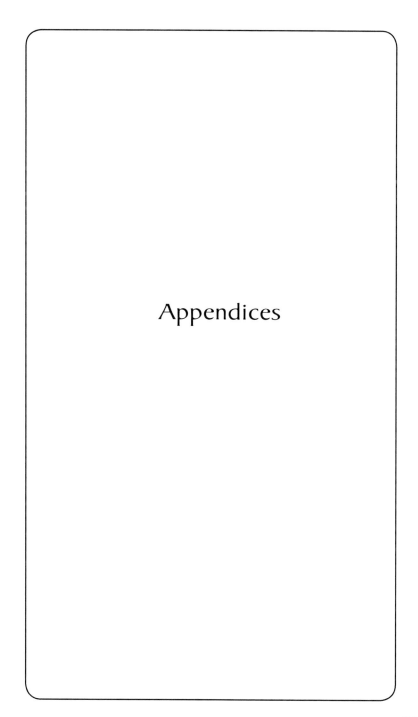

Appendices

Table: Coin Sequences and Passages

Truth	1	HHHHH	THHHH	33	Guile
Lust	2	HHHHT	THHHT	34	Celibacy
Love	3	HHHTH	THHTH	35	Bliss
Hope	4	HHHTT	THHTT	36	Vocation
Evil	5	HHTHH	THHTHH	37	Betrayal
Gestation	6	HHTHT	THHTHT	38	Kindness
Vigil	7	HHTTH	THHTTH	39	Death
Peace	8	HHTTT	THHTTT	40	Polarity
Renewal	9	HHTHHH	THTHHH	41	Generosity
Grace	10	HHTHHT	THTHHT	42	Mystery
Sublimity	11	HHTHTH	THTHTH	43	Patience
Hatred	12	HHTHTT	THTHTT	44	Vanity
Loss	13	HHTTHH	THTTHH	45	Reality
Deliverance	14	HHTTHT	THTTHT	46	Consciousness
Fright/Terror	15	HHTTTH	THTTTH	47	Life
Resolve	16	HHTTTT	THTTTT	48	Restoration
Heart	17	HTHHH	TTHHH	49	Repentance
Transition	18	HTHHHT	TTHHHT	50	Perdition
Transcendence	19	HTHHTH	TTHHTH	51	Compassion
Anger	20	HTHHTT	TTHHTT	52	Legacy
Rejection	21	HTHTHH	TTHTHH	53	Creativity
Innocence	22	HTHTHT	TTHTHT	54	Providence
Stewardship	23	HTHTTH	TTHTTH	55	Judgment
Loneliness	24	HTHTTT	TTHTTT	56	Promise
Honesty	25	HTTHHH	TTTHHH	57	Rebuff
Rest	26	HTTHHT	TTTHHT	58	Indifference
Freedom	27	HTTHTH	TTTHTH	59	Vulnerability
Despair	28	HTTHTT	TTTHTT	60	Community
Attachment	29	HTTTHH	TTTTHH	61	Dignity
Nurturance	30	HTTTHT	TTTTHT	62	Eloquence
Emptiness	31	HTTTTH	TTTTTH	63	Completion
Anticipation	32	HTTTTT	TTTTTT	64	The Unknowable

Table: Living Oracle–I Ching Correspondences[1]

Living Oracle Passage		I Ching Hexagram
#1 TRUTH	⇔	1. Ch'ien The Creative
#2 LUST (CRAVING)	⇔	43. Kuai Break-through (Resoluteness)
#3 LOVE	⇔	14. Ta Yu Possession in Great Measure
#4 HOPE	⇔	34. Ta Chuang The Power of the Great
#5 EVIL	⇔	9. Hsiao Ch'u The Taming power of the Small
#6 GESTATION	⇔	5. Hsu Waiting (Nourishment)
#7 VIGIL	⇔	26. Ta Ch'u The Taming Power of the Great
#8 PEACE	⇔	11. T'ai Peace
#9 RENEWAL	⇔	10 Lü Treading
#10 GRACE	⇔	58. Tui Joy
#11 SUBLIMITY	⇔	38. K'uei Opposition
#12 HATRED	⇔	54. Kuei Mei The Marrying Maiden
#13 LOSS	⇔	61. Chung Fu Inner Truth
#14 DELIVERANCE	⇔	60. Chieh Limitation

---

[1] These are the correspondences between *The Living Oracle* and the *I Ching*, used, during a consultation, in conjunction with *Relevant Passages*.

Living Oracle Passage		I Ching Hexagram
#15 FRIGHT / TERROR	⇔	41. Sun Decrease
#16 RESOLVE	⇔	19. Lin Approach
#17 HEART	⇔	13. T'ung Jên Fellowship with Men
#18 TRANSITION	⇔	49. Ko Revolution (Molting)
#19 TRANSCENDENCE	⇔	30. Li The Clinging, Fire
#20 ANGER	⇔	55. Fêng Abundance
#21 REJECTION	⇔	37. Chia Jên The Family (Clan)
#22 INNOCENCE	⇔	63. Chi Chi After Completion
#23 STEWARDSHIP	⇔	22. Pi Grace
#24 LONELINESS	⇔	36 Ming I Darkening of the Light
#25 HONESTY	⇔	25. Wu Wang Innocence (The Unexpected)
#26 REST	⇔	17. Sui Following
#27 FREEDOM	⇔	21. Shih Ho Biting Through
#28 DESPAIR	⇔	51. Chên The Arousing (Shock, Thunder)

Living Oracle Passage		I Ching Hexagram
#29 ATTACHMENT	⇔	42. I Increase
#30 NUTURANCE	⇔	3. Chun Difficulty at the Beginning
#31 EMPTINESS	⇔	27. I The Corners of the Mouth (Providing Nourishment)
#32 ANTICIPATION	⇔	24. Fu Return (The Turning Point)
#33 GUILE	⇔	44. Kou Coming to Meet
#34 CELIBACY (ABSTINENCE)	⇔	28. Ta Kuo Preponderance of the Great
#35 BLISS	⇔	50. Ting The Cauldron
#36 VOCATION (CALLING)	⇔	32. Hêng Duration
#37 BETRAYAL	⇔	57. Sun The Gentle (The Penetrating, Wind)
#38 KINDNESS (GOOD WILL)	⇔	48. Ching The Well
#39 DEATH	⇔	18. Ku Work on What Has Been Spoiled (Decay)
#40 POLARITY	⇔	46. Shêng Pushing Upward
#41 GENEROSITY	⇔	6. Sung Conflict
#42 MYSTERY	⇔	47. K'un Oppression (Exhaustion)
#43 PATIENCE	⇔	64. Wei Chi Before Completion

Living Oracle Passage		I Ching Hexagram
#44 VANITY	⇔	40. Hsieh Deliverance
#45 REALITY	⇔	59. Huan Dispersion (Dissolution)
#46 CONSCIOUSNESS	⇔	29. K'an The Abysmal (Water)
#47 LIFE	⇔	4. Mêng Youthful Folly
#48 RESTORATION	⇔	7. Shih The Army
#49 REPENTANCE	⇔	33. Tun Retreat
#50 PERDITION (DAMNATION)	⇔	31. Hsien Influence (Wooing)
#51 COMPASSION	⇔	56. Lü The Wanderer
#52 LEGACY	⇔	62. Hsiao Kuo Preponderance of the Small
#53 CREATIVITY	⇔	53. Chien Development (Gradual Progress)
#54 PROVIDENCE	⇔	39. Chien Obstruction
#55 JUDGEMENT (ASSESSMENT)	⇔	52. Kên Keeping Still, Mountain
#56 PROMISE (FULFILLEMENT)	⇔	15. Ch'ien Modesty
#57 REBUFF	⇔	12. P'i Standstill
#58 INDIFFERENCE	⇔	45. Ts'ui Gathering Together
#59 VULNERABILITY	⇔	35. Chin Progress

Living Oracle Passage		I Ching Hexagram
#60 COMMUNITY	⇔	16. Yü Enthusiasm
#61 DIGNITY	⇔	20. Kuan Contemplation (View)
#62 ELOQUENCE	⇔	8. Pi Holding Together (Union)
#63 COMPLETION (FULLNESS)	⇔	23. Po Splitting Apart
#64 THE UNKNOWABLE	⇔	2. K'un The Receptive

On Methodology and Probabilities

For those of you who are interested in the methodology involved in evoking passages in the course of a consultation, and want to follow the process of selection during the coin tosses (which can heighten the suspense during a consultation), here is how the process works:

The short rule governing the selection process is that with each cast of the coin the "Universe," which always has 64 slices at the outset of a consultation, is divided in half. Heads is always assigned to eliminate the higher-numbered half of the range of the prior "universe," while tails is always assigned to eliminate the lower-numbered half of the range. With each successive cast, the remaining "universe" pertaining to the inquiry is narrowed until, with the sixth cast, all that is left is a single passage. We can show this process of elimination with a an example, for instance, the sequence THHHTH. We start with the complete "Universe" of possibilities:

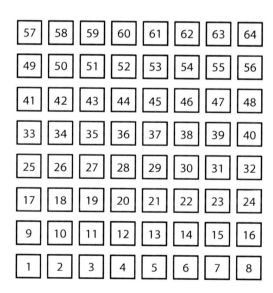

The first cast of (T)HHHTH is tails which, according to our elimination rule, removes 1-32 as shown on the following page:

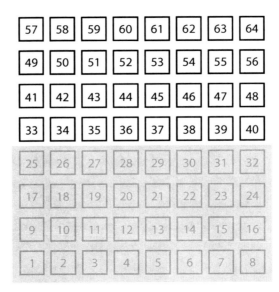

The second cast of T(H)HHTH, heads, eliminates the higher-numbered half of what is left:

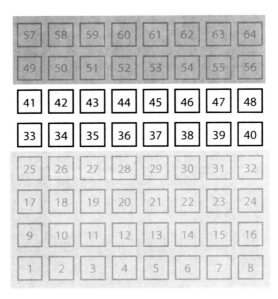

Using the same rules, the next four casts are (H)(H)(T)(H):

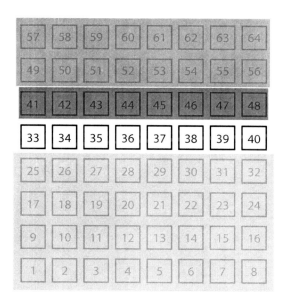

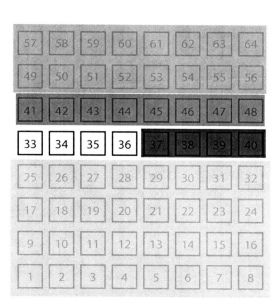

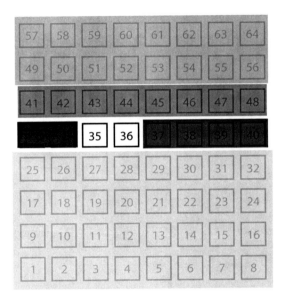

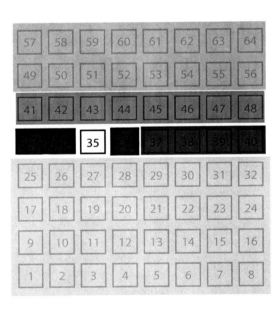

The final cast, heads, eliminates the higher-numbered half of the remaining Universe, leaving us with the selection of passage #35 BLISS.

As an additional aid, the following "decision tree" should help you to conceptualize the probabilities involved in the eliciting of passages via the coin method.

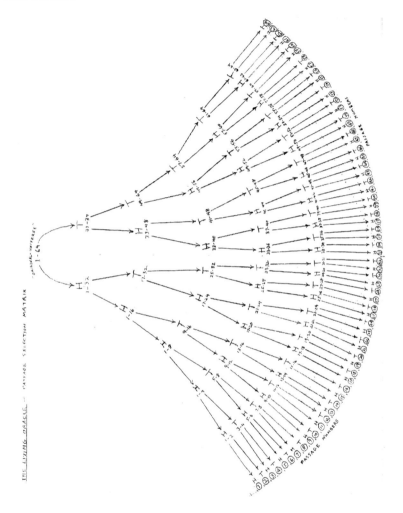

Regarding the overall probabilities involved in the eliciting of "one-passage," "two-passage" and "three-, four- or five-passage" readings, the probabilities involved with these various consultations are as follows:

The probability of receiving any given passage in a "one passage" reading is 1:64 (1.56%). For a two passage reading, the odds of obtaining any given two-passage sequence are 1:4,096 (0.02%). For readings involving the eliciting of the three temporally related passages (including, if desired, the one or two *Relevant Passages* [along with their *I Ching* correspondences] all of which follow as functions of the selection process of the first three passages) the probability of receiving any specific sequence is 1:262,144 (0.0004%).

List of Selected Readings

Divination and oracles

Archer, Stephen. *The Illustrated Encyclopedia of Divination*. Rockport, MA: Element Books, 1997.

Oracles and the developmental history of human consciousness

Jayne's, Julian. *The Origin of Consciousness in the Breakdown of the Bicameral Mind*. Boston: Houghton Mifflin, 1990.

Attributes of mystical consciousness

Huxley, Aldous, *The Perennial Philosophy*. New York: Harper Colophon, 1970.

James, William, *Varieties of Religious Experience*. New York: Touchstone/Simon & Schuster, 1997.

Quantum mechanics, synchronicity and non-locality

Albert, David Z. & Rivka Galchen,. "A Quantum Threat to Special Relativity." *Scientific American* 300 (3): 32-39.

Briggs, John P., Ph.D. & F. David Peat, Ph.D. *Looking Glass Universe: The Emerging Science of Wholeness*. New York: Touchstone/Simon & Schuster, 1984.

Capra, Frito. *The Tao of Physics*. Boston: Shambhala, 1991.

Dossey, Larry, M.D. *Healing Words: The Power of Prayer and the Practice of Medicine*. New York: HarperSanFrancisco, 1993.

Jung, C. G. *Synchronicity: An Acausal Connecting Principle.* From *The Collected Works of C. G. Jung.* No. 8. (Bollingen Ser.: No. XX). Princeton, NJ: Princeton University Press, 1973.

Wilber, Ken (ed). *The Holographic Paradigm and Other Paradoxes.* New York: Random House, 1995.

Zukav, Gary. *The Dancing Wu Li Masters.* New York: Bantam, 1984.

The I Ching

Benson, Robert D., (ed). *I Ching for a New Age: The Book of Answers for Changing Times.* Garden City Park, NY: Square One Publishers, 2002.

Cleary, Thomas (tr). *The Taoist I Ching.* Boston: Shambhala, 1986.

Siu, R. G. H. *The Portable Dragon: The Western Man's Guide to the I Ching.* Cambridge, MA: MIT Press, 1968.

Wilhelm, Richard. *The I Ching or Book of Changes.* Tr. from the German by C.F. Baynes. Foreword by C. G. Jung. (Bollingen Ser. No. XIX). Princeton, NJ: Princeton University Press, 1990.

Wing, R. L. *The I Ching Workbook.* New York: Doubleday, 1979.

The Runes

Blum, Ralph. *The Book of Runes.* New York: Oracle Books/St. Martin's Press, 1987.

Meadows, Kenneth. *Rune Power: The Secret Knowledge of the Wise Ones.* Rockport, MA: Earth Quest/Element Books, 1996.

The Tarot

Akron, & Hajo Banzhaf. *The Crowley Tarot: The Handbook to the Cards by Aleister Crowley and Lady Frieda Harris.* Stamford, CT: U. S. Games, 1995.

Echols, Signe E., Robert Mueller & Sandra A. Thomson. *Spiritual Tarot: Seventy-Eight Paths to Personal Development.* New York: Avon, 1996.

Sharman-Burke, Juliet. *The Complete Book of Tarot.* New York: St Martin's Press, 1985.

Sharman-Burke, Juliet & Liz Greene. *The Mythic Tarot: A New Approach to the Tarot.* New York: Fireside/Simon & Schuster, 1986.

Notes

Notes

Notes

Breinigsville, PA USA
10 September 2009
223815BV00006B/2/P